PENPALS

for

Handwriting

Year 1 Teacher's Book
(5–6 years)

Gill Budgell   Kate Ruttle

Series Consultants
Sue Palmer   Professor Rhona Stainthorp

Contents

CAMBRIDGE HITACHI

www.cambridge-hitachi.com

Scope and sequence

Foundation 1 / 3–5 years

DEVELOPING GROSS MOTOR SKILLS
1 The vocabulary of movement
2 Large movements
3 Responding to music

DEVELOPING FINE MOTOR SKILLS
4 Hand and finger play   6 Links to art
5 Making and modelling   7 Using one-handed tools and equipment

DEVELOPING PATTERNS AND BASIC LETTER MOVEMENTS
8 Pattern-making   12 Investigating circles
9 Responding to music   13 Investigating angled patterns
10 Investigating straight line patterns   14 Investigating eights and spirals
11 Investigating loops

Foundation 2 / Primary 1

Term 2
1 Introducing long ladder letters: *l, i, t, u, j, y*
2 Practising long ladder letters: *l, i*
3 Practising long ladder letters: *t, u*
4 Practising long ladder letters: *j, y*
5 Practising all the long ladder letters
6 Introducing one-armed robot letters: *r, b, n, h, m, k, p*
7 Practising one-armed robot letters: *b, n*
8 Practising one-armed robot letters: *h, m*
9 Practising one-armed robot letters: *k, p*
10 Practising all the one-armed robot letters
11 Introducing capitals for one-armed robot letters: *R, B, N, H, M, K, P*
12 Introducing capitals for long ladder letters: *L, I, T, U, J, Y*

Term 3
13 Introducing curly caterpillar letters: *c, a, d, o, s, g, q, e, f*
14 Practising curly caterpillar letters: *a, d*
15 Practising curly caterpillar letters: *o, s*
16 Practising curly caterpillar letters: *g, q*
17 Practising curly caterpillar letters: *e, f*
18 Practising all the curly caterpillar letters
19 Introducing zig-zag monster letters: *z, v, w, x*
20 Practising zig-zag monster letters: *v, w, x*
21 Introducing capitals for curly caterpillar letters: *C, A, D, O, S, G, Q, E, F*
22 Introducing capitals for zig-zag monster letters: *Z, V, W, X*
23 Exploring *ch, th* and *sh*

Year 1 / Primary 2

Term 1
1 Letter formation practice: long ladder family
2 Letter formation practice: one-armed robot family
3 Letter formation practice: curly caterpillar family
4 Letter formation practice: zig-zag monster family
5 Practising the vowels: *i*
6 Practising the vowels: *u*
7 Practising the vowels: *a*
8 Practising the vowels: *o*
9 Practising the vowels: *e*
10 Letter formation practice: capital letters

Term 2
11 Introducing diagonal join to ascender: joining *at, all*
12 Practising diagonal join to ascender: joining *th*
13 Practising diagonal join to ascender: joining *ch*
14 Practising diagonal join to ascender: joining *cl*
15 Introducing diagonal join, no ascender: joining *in, im*
16 Practising diagonal join, no ascender: joining *cr, tr, dr*
17 Practising diagonal join, no ascender: joining *lp, mp*
18 Introducing diagonal join, no ascender, to an anticlockwise letter: joining *id, ig*
19 Practising diagonal join, no ascender, to an anticlockwise letter: joining *nd, ld*
20 Practising diagonal join, no ascender, to an anticlockwise letter: joining *ng*

Term 3
21 Practising diagonal join, no ascender: joining *ee*
22 Practising diagonal join, no ascender: joining *ai, ay*
23 Practising diagonal join, no ascender: joining *ime, ine*
24 Introducing horizontal join, no ascender: joining *op, oy*
25 Practising horizontal join, no ascender: joining *one, ome*
26 Introducing horizontal join, no ascender, to an anticlockwise letter: joining *oa, og*
27 Practising horizontal join, no ascender, to an anticlockwise letter: joining *wa, wo*
28 Introducing horizontal join to ascender: joining *ol, ot*
29 Practising horizontal join to ascender: joining *wh, oh*
30 Introducing horizontal and diagonal joins to ascender, to an anticlockwise letter: joining *of, if*
31 Assessment

Year 2 / Primary 3

Term 1
1 How to join in a word: high-frequency words
2 Introducing the break letters: *j, g, x, y, z, b, f, p, q, r, s*
3 Practising diagonal join to ascender in words: *eel, eet*
4 Practising diagonal join, no ascender, in words: *a_e*
5 Practising diagonal join, no ascender, to an anticlockwise letter in words: *ice, ide*
6 Practising horizontal join, no ascender, in words: *ow, ou*
7 Practising horizontal join, no ascender, in words: *oy, oi*
8 Practising horizontal join, no ascender, to an anticlockwise letter in words: *oa, ode*
9 Practising horizontal join to ascender in words: *ole, obe*
10 Practising horizontal join to ascender in words: *ook, ool*

Term 2
11 Practising diagonal join to r: *ir, ur, er*
12 Practising horizontal join to r: *or, oor*
13 Introducing horizontal join from r to ascender: *url, irl, irt*
14 Introducing horizontal join from r: *ere*
15 Practising joining to and from r: *air*
16 Introducing diagonal join to s: *dis*
17 Introducing horizontal join to s: *ws*
18 Introducing diagonal join from s to ascender: *sh*
19 Introducing diagonal join from s, no ascender: *si, su, se, sp, sm*
20 Introducing horizontal join from r to an anticlockwise letter: *rs*

Term 3
21 Practising diagonal join to an anticlockwise letter: *ea, ear*
22 Introducing horizontal join to and from f to ascender: *ft, fl*
23 Introducing horizontal join from f, no ascender: *fu, fr*
24 Introducing *qu* (diagonal join, no ascender)
25 Introducing *rr* (horizontal join, no ascender)
26 Introducing *ss* (diagonal join, no ascender, to an anticlockwise letter)
27 Introducing *ff* (horizontal join to ascender)
28 Capital letter practice: height of ascenders and capitals
29 Assessment
30 Assessment

Scope and sequence

Year 3/Primary 4

Term 1
1 Revising joins in a word: long vowel phonemes
2 Revising joins in a word: *le*
3 Revising joins in a word: *ing*
4 Revising joins in a word: high-frequency words
5 Revising joins in a word: new vocabulary
6 Revising joins in a word: *un*, *de*
7 Revising joins to and from s: *dis*
8 Revising joins to and from r: *re*, *pre*
9 Revising joins to and from f: *ff*
10 Revising joins: *qu*

Term 2
11 Introducing joining b and p: diagonal join, no ascender, *bi*, *bu*, *pi*, *pu*
12 Practising joining b and p: diagonal join, no ascender, to an anticlockwise letter, *ba*, *bo*, *pa*, *po*
13 Practising joining b and p: diagonal join to ascender, *bl*, *ph*
14 Relative sizes of letters: silent letters
15 Parallel ascenders: high-frequency words
16 Parallel descenders: adding *y* to words
17 Relative size and consistency: *ly*, *less*, *ful*
18 Relative size and consistency: capitals
19 Speed and fluency practice: *er*, *est*
20 Speed and fluency practice: opposites

Term 3
21 Consistency in spacing: *mis*, *anti*, *ex*
22 Consistency in spacing: *non*, *co*
23 Consistency in spacing: apostrophes
24 Layout, speed and fluency practice: address
25 Layout, speed and fluency practice: dialogue
26 Layout, speed and fluency practice: poem
27 Layout, speed and fluency practice: letter
28 Handwriting style
29 Assessment
30 Handwriting style

Year 4/Primary 5

Term 1
1 Revising joins in a word: *ness*, *ship*
2 Revising joins in a word: *ing*, *ed*
3 Revising joins in a word: *s*
4 Revising joins in a word: *ify*
5 Revising joins in a word: *nn*, *mm*, *ss*
6 Revising parallel ascenders: *tt*, *ll*, *bb*
7 Revising parallel ascenders and descenders: *pp*, *ff*
8 Revising joins to an anticlockwise letter: *cc*, *dd*
9 Revising break letters: alphabetical order
10 Linking spelling and handwriting: related words

Term 2
11 Introducing sloped writing
12 Parallel ascenders: *al*, *ad*, *af*
13 Parallel descenders and break letters: *ight*, *ough*
14 Size, proportion and spacing: *ious*
15 Size, proportion and spacing: *able*, *ful*
16 Size, proportion and spacing: *fs*, *ves*
17 Speed and fluency: abbreviations for notes
18 Speed and fluency: notemaking
19 Speed and fluency: drafting
20 Speed and fluency: lists

Term 3
21 Size, proportion and spacing: *v*, *k*
22 Size, proportion and spacing: *ic*, *ist*
23 Size, proportion and spacing: *ion*
24 Size, proportion and spacing: contractions
25 Speed and fluency: *ible*, *able*
26 Speed and fluency: diminutives
27 Print alphabet
28 Print capitals
29 Assessment
30 Presentational skills: font styles

Years 5 & 6/Primary 6 & 7

Year 5 Handwriting
1 Revision: practising sloped writing
2 Revision: practising the joins
3 Developing style for speed: joining from *t*
4 Developing style for speed: looping from *g*, *j* and *y*
5 Developing style for speed: joining from *f*
6 Developing style for speed: joining from *s*
7 Developing style for speed: writing *v*, *w*, *x* and *z* at speed
8 Developing style for speed: pen breaks in longer words
9 Different styles for different purposes
10 Assessment

Year 5 Project work
11 Haiku project: making notes
12 Haiku project: organising ideas
13 Haiku project: producing a draft
14 Haiku project: publishing the haiku
15 Haiku project: evaluation
16 Letter project: making notes
17 Letter project: structuring an argument
18 Letter project: producing a draft
19 Letter project: publishing a letter
20 Letter project: evaluation

Year 6 Handwriting
21 Self-assessment: evaluating handwriting
22 Self-assessment: checking the joins
23 Self-assessment: consistency of size
24 Self-assessment: letters resting on baseline
25 Self-assessment: ascenders and descenders
26 Self-assessment: consistency of size of capitals and ascenders
27 Writing at speed: inappropriate closing of letters
28 Writing at speed: identifying unclosed letters
29 Writing at speed: spacing within words
30 Writing at speed: spacing between words

Year 6 Project work
31 Playscript project: collecting information
32 Playscript project: recording ideas
33 Playscript project: producing a draft
34 Playscript project: publishing a playscript
35 Playscript project: evaluation
36 Information notice project: collecting and organising information
37 Information notice project: organising information
38 Information notice project: producing a draft
39 Information notice project: publishing a notice
40 Information notice project: evaluation

Penpals rationale

Even in this computer-literate age, good handwriting remains fundamental to our children's educational achievement. *Penpals for Handwriting* will help you teach children to develop fast, fluent, legible handwriting. The rationale for introducing joining is fully explained on page 12. This carefully structured handwriting scheme can also make a difference to overall attainment in writing.

Traditional principles in the contemporary classroom

We believe that:

1 A flexible, fluent and legible handwriting style empowers children to write with confidence and creativity. This is an entitlement that needs skilful teaching.

2 Handwriting is a developmental process with its own distinctive stages of sequential growth. We have identified five stages that form the basic organisational structure of *Penpals*:

1 Readiness for handwriting; gross and fine motor skills leading to letter formation (Foundation / 3–5 years)

2 Beginning to join (Key Stage 1 / 5–7 years)

3 Securing the joins (Key Stage 1 and lower Key Stage 2 / 5–9 years)

4 Practising speed and fluency (lower Key Stage 2 / 7–9 years)

5 Presentation skills (upper Key Stage 2 / 10–11 years)

3 Handwriting must be actively taught: this can be done in association with spelling. Learning to associate the kinaesthetic handwriting movement with the visual letter pattern and the aural phonemes will help children with learning to spell.

Whilst the traditional skills of handwriting still need to be taught, these skills now have to be delivered within a new curriculum.

Handwriting lessons can link effectively with early phonic and spelling work that will be happening in the classroom in the same term. *Penpals* fully exploits these overlap opportunities.

A practical approach

Penpals offers a practical approach to aid the delivery of handwriting teaching in the context of the modern curriculum:

● **Time** *Penpals'* focus on whole-class teaching, with key teaching points clearly identified, allows effective teaching in the time available.

● **Planning** *Penpals* helps with long-, medium- and short-term planning for each key stage, correlated to national guidelines.

● **Practice** *Penpals* offers pupil Practice Books with their own internal structure of excellent models for finger tracing and independent writing.

● **Revision** *Penpals* offers opportunities for record-keeping, review and assessment throughout the course.

● **Motivation** The *Penpals* materials are attractive and well designed with the support of handwriting experts to stimulate and motivate children.

● **ICT** Use the *Penpals* CD-ROMs to enrich and extend children's handwriting experiences.

A few words from the experts...

Professor Rhona Stainthorp *Professor, Institute of Education, University of Reading*

We now know that if children are to achieve comfortable, legible, flexible handwriting styles, they need to be taught to form and join each letter efficiently. *Penpals* sets out to achieve this. Children need good models to copy, lots of practice and feedback to help them fine-tune their performance. This is

accepted pedagogy in sport and music and we now know that it is also essential if children are to learn to write with legibility and speed. Legibility is important in order to communicate to others and to read one's own texts. Speed is essential so that the translation of thoughts into texts is not held back by the production of the letters.

If the practice element of letter formation includes the practice of spelling patterns, as in *Penpals*, the resultant pedagogy addresses two of the essential sub-skills of good written communication, namely handwriting and spelling.

Efficient handwriting leads to higher-quality writing.

Dr Rosemary Sassoon *Handwriting expert*

The Sassoon family of typefaces has been used throughout this scheme. Many people might therefore describe them as the model but they are typefaces, not exactly a handwriting model. No hand could copy them exactly and be so consistent and invariable. Equally, no typeface, however many alternative letters and joins are built in to a font, can be quite as flexible as handwritten letters. Our letters represent the movement, proportions and clear characteristics of basic separate and joined letters. It is likely that every teacher will produce his or her own slightly different version on the whiteboard, and pupils will then do likewise. It matters little if the slant or proportions of a child's writing differ slightly from any model. We are not teaching children to be forgers. We are equipping them with an efficient, legible handwriting that will serve them all their life – one that suits their hand and their personality. Flexibility is stressed throughout this scheme.

Links to national guidelines

Penpals Year 1/Primary 2 supports many National Guidelines including:

- *The National Curriculum for England and Wales*;
- *Primary Framework for literacy and mathematics* (Primary National Strategy 2006);
- *Letters and sounds – Principles and Practice of High Quality Phonics* (DfES 2007);
- *English Language 5–14 Guidelines* (The Scottish Office Education Department);
- *The Northern Ireland Curriculum: Primary* (CCEA).

Penpals and phonics

Penpals gives children the opportunity to revisit and consolidate their growing knowledge of phonics and spelling while securing the kinaesthetic movements needed for a legible, fast and fluent handwriting style.

In the *Penpals* Foundation 2, Year 1 and Year 2 CD-ROMs the word banks give opportunities for learning handwriting in the context of words that are easy to read and spell. After each handwriting movement has been introduced and practised it is recommended you revise the movement with a clear phonics focus in line with the appropriate *Letters and sounds* phase.

By Year 3 the transition from phonics into spelling has been made. All of the screens in the *Penpals* Year 3, Year 4 and Years 5 & 6 CD-ROMs create opportunities to revisit and secure spelling patterns while developing a confident and fluent handwriting style.

The chart links the units in the *Penpals* Year 1 CD-ROM with additional phonics practice. Also included in this chart are some high-frequency words that will be useful for practising spelling and for developing handwriting.

Year	*Letters and sounds* phase	*Penpals* Year 1 CD-ROM unit	Phonic words including high-frequency decodable words	High-frequency tricky and decodable words for additional practice
Year 1	5	1–4 *letter formation*	skip, think, hand, this, lost, spring, lunch, crash, stamp, print	going, said, so, like, some, come, there, little, one, out
		5–9 *vowel formation*	make, sail, these, three, like, right, home, coat, rule, blew	day, they, she, see, time, by, don't, old, do, too
		11–14 *diagonal join to ascender*	help, little, liked, these, back, pull, clear, each, put, animal	at, but, the, their, there, children, water, want, school, only
		15–17 *diagonal join, no ascender*	shape, paint, spray, geese, three, climb, shine, crime, pie, shy	said, come, again, friend, have, day, time, here, saw, away
		18–20 *diagonal join to anticlockwise letter*	asked, do, please, light, ground, slide, thing, treat, string, gold	do, asked, looked, home, some, thing, sea, place, across, really
		24–25 *horizontal join, no ascender*	come, one, out, looked, mouse, house, know, noise, word, wrong	some, for, you, one, down, come, now, about, your, could
		26–27 *horizontal join to anticlockwise letter*	log, code, roast, throat, cloak, choose, spoon, goose, screws, away	was, we, went, were, looked, too, good, water, was, won
		28–29 *horizontal join to ascender*	while, whale, white, globe, whole, note, clothes, joke, cold, wheel	when, what, old, oh, old, school, clothes, mother, other, looking
		30 *horizontal join to ascender of anticlockwise letter*	off, office, take-off, toffee, snowflake, awful, hoof, offer, roof, waterproof	of, soft, often

Note: Underlining is used to show joins.

Classroom organisation

The ideal classroom organisation for teaching *Penpals* is to have the children sitting at desks or tables arranged so that they can all see the interactive white board (IWB). Each child needs a dry-wipe board (preferably with guidelines) and a marker pen or pencil and paper.

If this organisation is not possible within your classroom, bear in mind the following points as you plan your own classroom:

- All the children need to see the IWB and be able to copy words or handwriting patterns from it.
- Handwriting is usually done on a horizontal or slightly sloped surface.

When to use *Penpals*

Penpals can be used flexibly to teach handwriting. Ideally the whole-class teaching session will be followed immediately by the independent work, but where this is not possible the sessions may be split.

Timing the sessions

The whole-class session for each unit, including the warm-up activities, should take no more than 15 minutes. The independent working session should take about 15–20 minutes.

In addition to the allocated time, extra daily 'practice times' of 5–10 minutes are ideal.

Penpals for Handwriting: Y1 © Gill Budgell (Frattempo) and Kate Ruttle 2009

Sequence for teaching the units

Gross and fine motor skills

The progression of the Foundation and Key Stage 1 lessons is generally assumed to be that of moving from gross to fine motor skills.

Teaching units

In *Penpals: Y1/P2* 10 units have been provided for each school term, with one extra assessment unit in Term 3. The units have been organised into a specific teaching sequence to ensure that skills are developed, practised and consolidated and that relevant phonic and spelling practice can be used.

Teaching sequence for a unit of *Penpals for Handwriting*

You will need:

- the Year 1 CD-ROM;
- the relevant Teacher's Book page;
- the Big Book or water-based marker pens for annotating the pages.

Children will need:

- space for both gross and fine motor skill warm ups;
- dry-wipe boards and marker pens;*
- pencils and coloured pencils;
- the relevant Practice Book;
- handwriting exercise book.

(*Remember that one of the crucial elements of ensuring good handwriting is good posture. If children are writing with dry-wipe boards on their knees or on the floor, good posture is more difficult to achieve.)

Whole-class session

1 **Warm up** These ideas complement the gross and fine motor control warm-up clips accessible from the main menu of the CD-ROM. Use these at the start of the lesson to prepare the upper part of the body and the hands for handwriting.

2 **Unit focus and phonic/spelling link** These are clearly identified at the start of each unit.

4 **Sky writing** These involve children drawing patterns in the air. They are an ideal way of introducing a gross motor movement before refining it as a fine motor movement.

5 **Letter/join animations** These provide opportunities to demonstrate and talk about correct letter/join formation. Children can practise tracing and copying the letters/joins.

6 **Challenge word** Click on the toucan to reveal a challenge word related to the focus letter/join.

7 **Word bank** These activities provide banks of differentiated words that you can use to model and discuss letter/join formation. Children can practise tracing the target letter/joins in words.

3 **Units** Every unit begins with a whole-class teaching session based on the CD-ROM.

8 **Group work** Guidance for using the Big Book page with small groups to reinforce modelling the focus letters/joins in the context of longer texts.

10 **Independent work** See page 7.

9 **Common errors** Joining issues to look out for while children are working.

Independent work

This session can follow on directly from the whole-class session. Alternatively, it can be completed in other literacy time. Ideally, the children's work should be overseen by an adult to ensure correct formation and joining. The teacher's page for the unit provides helpful advice on using the Practice Book page together and highlights some common errors to look out for.

At Key Stage 1 and Key Stage 2, children will need a handwriting exercise book to record their work in. They should have a sharpened pencil for their writing, but may also need coloured pencils for pattern practice.

The Practice Book pages offer:

1 **Finger tracing** Red letters to indicate the focus letter or join.

2 **Independent writing** Practising the focus letter or join.

3 **Copying letters in context** Once the children have practised writing the letters or joins, they should try to write them in a context (usually a simple phrase or sentence, joke or rhyme). Familiarity with the correct formation of all patterns and letters is expected. (If necessary, *Penpals: Foundation 2* may be referred to for revision or consolidation.)

5 **Pattern practice** Children will need to practise the patterns at the bottom of the page. These usually reflect the pencil movement of the unit focus, but always enhance fine motor control. These patterns can be made using coloured pencils. These patterns are artwork, not letters, and should be treated as opportunities to develop movement and control.

4 **High-frequency words** Look, Say, Cover, Write, Check practice is provided for high-frequency words that feature the unit focus join (where possible).

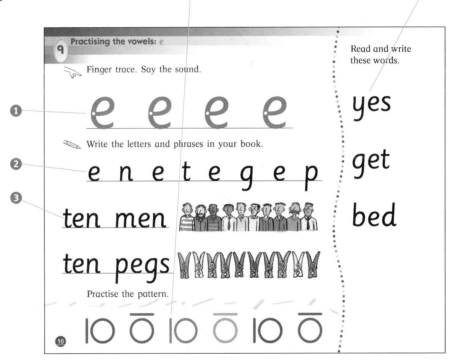

Also in the Teacher's Book:

Take aways These are photocopy masters (PCMs) for extra practice or homework. In addition to a PCM consolidating the unit focus, Units 1–10 direct you back to a PCM in F2 for additional letter formation practice for children who need reinforcement.

Differentiation

Differentiation using *Penpals* can be achieved in a number of ways:

- Children working individually with a Teaching Assistant may benefit from additional practice on dry-wipe boards.
- Take away activities provide excellent opportunities for differentiation as detailed above. Cross-references to similar Take aways in earlier books can help you to select less challenging activities for those who need extra practice at a lower level.
- Higher-achieving children can be challenged by higher expectations of control and evenness of letters. They may also be able to transfer joins between sessions.

Assessment and record-keeping

On-going formative assessment

The most effective assessment of handwriting is on-going assessment because this gives you the chance to spot any errors or inconsistencies that are likely to impede a fast, fluent hand in the future. Be especially aware of left-handers and the difference between a pencil hold that will seriously limit their success in the future and one that has been found to work efficiently.

At Key Stage 1 a starting point assessment PCM is provided for use at the beginning of each school year (see page 9). This assesses the previous year's work and gives an indication of what needs to be consolidated before beginning new work.

On the teacher's page for every unit, the Common errors section draws attention to the most common mistakes children make.

The Practice Book page annotations also enable you to draw the children's attention to particular handwriting issues.

Summative assessment

Beginning of year

The PCM on page 9 can be used for an assessment to ensure that all children are ready for *Penpals: Y1/P2*. If children's letter formation is still insecure, they will benefit from revising units in *Penpals: Foundation 2*.

End of year

From Y1/P2 you can use text from the final unit in each book as the basis of a summative assessment. As you do the summative assessment, consider key handwriting issues:

- Are all letters formed correctly?
- Are letters consistently sized?
- Are known joins used?
- Are they used correctly?
- Are ascenders and descenders parallel?
- Are spaces within and between words regular?
- Is good handwriting carried over into cross-curricular activities?
- What are the next handwriting targets for this child?

Record-keeping

- The best record of what children have achieved will be in their handwriting books. It is therefore important to keep a book specifically for this purpose. This will provide a useful record of achievement to share with parents and colleagues.
- The Contents page can be photocopied and used with highlighting pens and dates to keep a record of which units have been completed. You may find it helpful to use a 'traffic light' system (green highlighter pen for 'achieved', yellow for 'not totally secure' and pink for 'not achieved') to highlight units you need to revisit with individuals, groups or the whole class.

Children's beginning of year assessment

Name ....   Date ....

Copy each letter in the space.

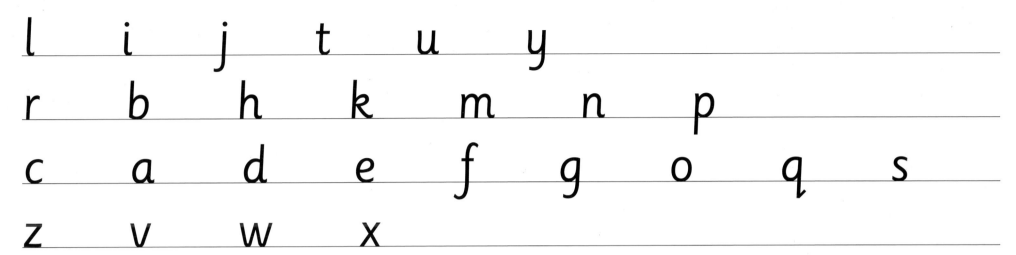

l   i   j   t   u   y

r   b   h   k   m   n   p

c   a   d   e   f   g   o   q   s

z   v   w   x

Now copy these patterns.

Glossary of key terms

Talking about handwriting

Throughout *Penpals* it has been assumed that correct terminology should be used as soon as possible. At Key Stage 1 there is an emphasis on talking about letter formation in the context of joining.

Terms used in *Penpals* include:

- **Lower case letter**.
- **Capital letter** is used in preference to 'upper case letter'.
- **Short letter** is the term used to describe a letter with no ascender or descender.
- **Letter with an ascender, letter with a descender.**
- **Flick** is used to describe an exit stroke (note that *t* finishes with a curl to the right rather than merely an exit flick).
- **Curve** is used to describe the descender on letters (*y, j, g, f*).
- **Cross bar** is used to describe the left-to-right line on *t* and *f*. It may also be used in relation to letters that feature a left-to-right horizontal line (e.g. *e* and *z*).
- **Diagonal join to ascender** (e.g. *at*), **diagonal join (no ascender)** (e.g. *du*), **diagonal join to an anticlockwise letter** (e.g. *ho*).
- **Horizontal join to ascender** (e.g. *oh*), **horizontal join (no ascender)** (e.g. *re*), **horizontal join to an anticlockwise letter** (e.g. *wo*).
- Other important terminology used throughout *Penpals* includes **vertical, parallel, joined, sloped, anticlockwise**.

Key CD-ROM features

- **Warm-up clips** These activities may be linked to the focus of the unit but are generally just enjoyable movement activities to warm up the muscles.
- **Sky writing** This means tracing patterns in the air, or on the carpet or table in front of you. Encourage children to use one of their fingers as a pointer for these activities.
- **Letter/join animations** These animations encourage the children to watch and sky write as the focus letter/join animates on the screen.
- **Word bank** This provides a useful bank of words that enable you to demonstrate the focus letters/joins.
- **Show alphabet** These animations show how to form all capital and lower case letters.

Notes on formation of specific letters and joins

Correct letter formation can be demonstrated using the **Show alphabet** section on the CD-ROM.

- *k* – the use of the curly form of *k*, as opposed to the straight *k* is recommended by handwriting experts because its flowing form lends itself more naturally to joining. It is also more easily distinguished from the capital letter.
- *o* – there is no exit stroke from the lower case *o* when it is not joined. Unlike the flick at the bottom of letters like *n* and *l*, the exit stroke from the *o* is not an integral part of the letter, but simply a mechanism for joining.
- *e* – two different forms of *e* (*e* and *ɛ*) are used in order to show children how it alters when other letters are joined to it.
- *b, f, p, q, r* and *s* are letters that the children are taught to join in later years.
- *g, j* and *y* are letters that don't join, although there is some exploration of joining them in Y5&6/P6&7.
- *x* and *z* are never joined to or from as these are uncomfortable joins that often result in the malformation of both the joining letter and the *x* or *z*. Also, handwriting is generally faster and more legible if it is not continuously joined.

Capital letters

Capitals are taught in the Foundation 2 materials and then revisited in subsequent years as appropriate. It is generally agreed that there is no right or wrong way to form capitals; however, we suggest they should be written from top to bottom and left to right wherever possible. As skills and confidence develop, left-handers may well form capitals differently (they have a tendency to go from right to left, for example). This should not be an issue as capitals are never joined.

- **Capital** *Y* – the use of a central stalk (as opposed to a slanting stalk) is recommended, as once children have completed the 'v' form at the top of the letter, they have a clear starting point for the downwards stroke. This formation also distinguishes the capital letter from the lower case letter and retains its shape when written at speed.
- **Capital** *G* – this form of *G* is recommended as the correct handwriting form of the letter. Variations which include a vertical line (*G*) are font forms.
- **Capital** *H* – the formation of *H* using two down strokes followed by the horizontal stroke from left to right is recommended. The alternative (one down stroke followed by a horizontal and a further down stroke) can quickly resemble the letter *M* when written at speed.
- **Capital** *K* – this formation of *K* (with two pencil strokes rather than three) is recommended as it is more fluently formed when writing at speed.

Letter patter for *Penpals*

This chart shows the oral patter for the formation of lower case and capital letters.

Long ladder family

l	Start at the top, come all the way down and flick.	L	Start at the top, come down and go across.
i	Start at the top, come down and flick. Lift and dot.	I	Start at the top, come down. Lift. Across at the top. Lift. Across at the bottom.
t	Start at the top, come all the way down and curve. Lift and cross.	T	Start at the top, come down. Lift. Across at the top.
u	Start at the top, come down and curve. Go back up, come back down and flick.	U	Start at the top, come down. Curve back up.
j	Start at the top, come all the way down and curve to the left. Lift and dot.	J	Start at the top, come down. Curve to the left. Lift. Across at the top.
y	Start at the top, come all the way down and curve. Go back up, come all the way down and curve to the left.	Y	Slope down, slope back up. Lift. Come down from the point.

One-armed robot family

r	Start at the top, come down, bounce back up and over.	R	Start at the top, come down. Lift. Back to the top. Go all the way round and slope.
b	Start at the top, come all the way down, bounce half-way back up and go all the way round.	B	Start at the top, come down. Lift. Back to the top. Go all the way round and all the way round again.
n	Start at the top, come down, bounce back up, go over, down and flick.	N	Start at the top, come down. Lift. Back to the top. Slope and straight up.
h	Start at the top, come all the way down, bounce half-way back up, go over, down and flick.	H	Start at the top, come down. Lift. Start at the top come down. Lift and across in the middle.
m	Start at the top, come down, bounce back up and over. Down, bounce back up and over. Down and flick.	M	Start at the top, come down. Lift. Back to the top. Slope down, slope up and straight down.
k or k	Start at the top, come all the way down, bounce half-way back up. Loop. Slope and flick. or Start at the top, come all the way down. Lift. Slope. Slope and flick.	K	Start at the top, come down. Lift. Slope in, slope out.
p	Start at the top, come all the way down, bounce back up and go all the way round.	P	Start at the top, come down. Lift. Back to the top. Go all the way round.

Curly caterpillar family

c	Make a curve.	C	Make a curve.
a	Make a curve, go up to the top, come back down and flick.	A	Slope to the left. Lift back to the top. Slope. Lift. Across in the middle.
d	Make a curve, go all the way up, come back down and flick.	D	Start at the top, come down. Lift. Back to the top. Go all the way round to the bottom.
o	Make a curve, go all the way round.	O	Make a curve, go all the way round.
s	Make a curve, slope, make a curve back again.	S	Make a curve, slope, make a curve back again.
g	Make a curve, go up to the top, come all the way down and curve to the left.	G	Make a curve. Lift and go across.
q	Make a curve, go up to the top, come all the way down and flick.	Q	Make a curve, go all the way round. Lift and slope across.
e	Start with a loop then make a curve.	E	Start at the top, come down. Lift. Back to the top. Across at the top. Lift. Across in the middle. Lift. Across at the bottom.
f	Make a curve, come all the way down, curve to the left. Lift and cross.	F	Start at the top, come down. Lift. Back to the top. Across at the top. Lift. Across in the middle.

Zig-zag monster family

z	Go across, slope, go back across.	Z	Go across, slope, go back across.
v	Slope down, slope back up.	V	Slope down, slope back up.
w	Slope down, slope back up. Slope down again and slope back up.	W	Slope down, slope back up. Slope down again and slope back up.
x	Slope. Lift and slope across.	X	Slope. Lift and slope across.

In order to promote fluent handwriting and to support the early stages of spelling, some handwriting joins are introduced in Y1/P2 as soon as all individual letter formation is secure.

Throughout the Key Stage 1 resources, new joins are introduced in a unit that presents a variety of words featuring those joins. In Y2/P3, children are given opportunities to practise joins that they have already learnt. Children are never expected to copy text featuring joins that they have not been formally taught.

Progression in the introduction of joins

Y1/P2 The main focus is on consolidating letter formation and introducing the language and movement of joining. For this reason, in these resources only two or three letters in a word are joined. The words on the CD-ROM and in the Big Book and the Practice Book feature the focus join for the teaching unit.

Transference and mixing of joins

In Y1/P2 transference of joins from one unit to another is not generally shown. As well as keeping the focus clearly on the target join, this prevents children being overwhelmed by joined sequences and mixtures of joins within the same word.

However, once *ch* and *th* have been introduced (Units 12 and 13), these letter combinations are always shown joined to support the phonic association taught in Foundation 2. (*sh* is taught in *Penpals: Y2/P3* as joins from *s* are more complex.)

Where children are ready to transfer other joins that they have previously learnt, encourage them to do so.

The sequence for *Penpals: Y1/P2* is:

- T1: Revising letter families and formations, including capitals.
- T2: Introducing and practising diagonal join to ascender

and no ascender (including diagonal join, no ascender to an anticlockwise letter).
- T3: Further practice of diagonal join, no ascender. Introducing horizontal join, no ascender, and to ascender (including joining to an anticlockwise letter).

Y2/P3 As more joins are introduced, children are given opportunities to practise familiar joins which are not the focus of the unit. During the year, children are expected to begin to join all the letters in a short word, or to join letter patterns which can support spelling.

Y3&4/P4&5 All the basic joins will now be familiar. In these resources, children are asked to practise 'tricky joins' and to begin to develop fluent, even handwriting. An emphasis on spacing between letters and words, consistency of letter size and parallel ascenders and descenders helps children to present their work well.

Y4/P5 Children are introduced to a sloped style of writing and are expected to write mostly in pen.

Y5&6/P6&7 Two sets of OHTs are provided for each of these year groups, one with a handwriting focus, the other with a project focus.

Defining the joins

(See the inside back cover of this Teacher's Book for a list of letter sets requiring each of the joins as taught in Y1/P2.)

The two basic join types

- **Diagonal join** (e.g. *at*) (introduced in Y1/P2, Unit 11): this is the most common join. It starts from the final flick on the baseline (or 'curl' in the case of the letter *t*). Letters which come before a diagonal join are: *a, c, d, e, h, i, k, l, m, n, t, u* (and *q*, which begins below the baseline).

- **Horizontal join** (e.g. *op*) (introduced in Y1/P2, Unit 24): this join is formed from letters which finish at the top of the letter rather than at the baseline. Letters which come before a horizontal join are: *o, v, w*.

Variations on the join types

Penpals uses three subsets of the main joins: join to a letter with an ascender, join to a letter with no ascender and join to a letter that begins with an anticlockwise movement. Since the last subset involves stopping the pencil and reversing the direction of movement, these are called *diagonal join to an anticlockwise letter* and *horizontal join to an anticlockwise letter*. Joins to anticlockwise letters are trickier to teach and need more practice than straightforward horizontal and diagonal joins. These joins tend to 'decay' when children begin to write more quickly.

- **Diagonal join to a letter with an ascender** (e.g. *ub*) (introduced in Y1/P2, Unit 11): this is a variation of the diagonal join.
- **Diagonal join to an anticlockwise letter** (e.g. *no*) (introduced in Y1/P2, Unit 18): joining with a diagonal join to the anticlockwise letters in the 'curly caterpillar' family involves stopping the hand movement and reversing it. This can be a tricky join and it decays easily in fast writing.
- **Horizontal join to an anticlockwise letter** (e.g. *wo*) (introduced in Y1/P2, Unit 26): joining from a horizontal join to an anticlockwise letter involves a reversal.
- **Horizontal join to a letter with an ascender** (e.g. *oh*) (introduced in Y1/P2, Unit 28): this is a slightly sloping version of a horizontal join.
- **Break letters** (introduced in Y2/P3): these are letters from which no join has yet been taught (see notes on page 10).

When you introduce *Penpals* into your school, it is important to ensure that all the staff in the school follow the scheme. To do this, it may be useful to hold an INSET staff meeting. The following pages in this book are photocopiable to make OHTs for this purpose:

- page 14 – outline of INSET session;
- page 15 – information sheet for parents;
- page 16 – variations of the font used in *Penpals*;
- pages 63 and 64 – handwriting mats;
- inside back cover – joining letter sets (also appears on the inside back cover of the Big Book and Practice Book).

Suggested topics for inclusion in INSET meeting

Organisational issues

- **Rationale for introducing *Penpals* for Handwriting** Use the information on page 4.
- **Classroom organisation** Copy page 5 of this introduction for all staff. Read through it together, agreeing on the most appropriate time for the sessions, etc.
- **Assessment and record-keeping** Use the information on page 8.
- **Home–school links** Make an OHT of the information sheet on page 14.

Handwriting issues

- **Font** Use the **Show alphabet** section on the CD-ROM to demonstrate the font. Information on page 10 of the introduction may be used to clarify any issues arising.
- **Font sizes** Photocopy page 16 of this Teacher's Book to demonstrate how font size is shown throughout *Penpals*.
- **Joins and break letters** Use the **Show joining letter sets** section on the CD-ROM, or an OHT of the inside back cover of this book, to demonstrate the joining letter sets and the break letters.
- **Writing on lined paper** Children should be encouraged to write on lined paper from the time they begin to focus on correct letter formation and orientation. As the children's handwriting becomes more controlled, the width between the lines should decrease. It may well be that at any given time different children in your class will benefit from writing on paper with different line widths. The size of the font in the Practice Books is intended to reflect a development in handwriting. However, you should still tailor the handwriting materials to meet the needs of individual children in your class. Some children may prefer to write on lined paper which also includes guidelines for the height of ascenders and descenders.
- **Pencil hold** Use the pencil hold videos in the **Posture clips** section on the CD-ROM to illustrate good pencil hold. The traditionally recommended pencil hold allows children to sustain handwriting for long periods without tiring their hands. However, there are many alternative pencil holds (particularly for left-handers) and the most important thing is comfort and a hold that will be efficient under speed. Some children may benefit from triangular pencils or ordinary pencils with plastic pencil grips.

- **Posture** Use the photographs in the **Posture clips** section on the CD-ROM to illustrate good posture. A good posture and pencil hold are vital for good handwriting. Although many young children enjoy sitting on one foot, kneeling or wrapping their feet around the legs of the chair, they will find it easier to sustain good handwriting comfortably if they adopt a good posture.
- **Left-handed children** Left-handed children should not sit to the right of right-handed children as their papers will meet in the middle! Left-handed children should be taught to position their paper to the left of centre and then angle the paper for comfort as suggested below. Use the left-handed pencil hold video and posture photograph in the **Posture clips** section on the CD-ROM to illustrate this. There is no reason why left-handed children's handwriting should be any worse than that of right-handed children.
- **Sloped surfaces** Children who experience some motor control difficulties often benefit from writing on a slight slope. The easiest and cheapest way to provide this in the classroom is to use substantial A4 or foolscap ring-binders of which there are usually plenty in school. Commercial wooden or plastic writing slopes are also widely available.
- **Angle of paper** Make an OHT of the guidelines for right- and left-handed children as provided on pages 63 and 64. You can photocopy these on to A3 paper and laminate them to make table-top mats for the children. Use the spaces provided to allow children to find the optimum position. Show the children how to line up the corners of their books to create a comfortable angle for writing, or how to use Blu-tack to secure paper to the mats to produce guidelines when writing on blank paper. These guidelines provide a good guide but encourage the children to explore personal variation of the angles.

Organisational issues

- ## Rationale
  - a flexible, fluent and legible handwriting style
  - a 5-stage developmental process
  - active teaching in association with phonics and spelling

- ## Classroom organisation
  - weekly teaching sessions with little-and-often practice

- ## Assessment and record keeping
  - beginning of year assessment for each year group encourages self-assessment

- ## Home-school links
  - parent information sheets for each year
  - homework activities

Handwriting issues
font, font size, joins and break letters, writing on lined paper, pencil hold, posture, left-handed children, sloped surfaces, angle of paper

Penpals for Handwriting: Year 1 information sheet for parents

Letter formation should now be becoming familiar and secure.

As a reminder, correct letter formation for lower case letters is as follows:

a, b, c, d, e, f, g, h, i, j, k, l, m, n, o, p, q, r, s, t, u, v, w, x, y, z

Capital letters are formed as follows:

A, B, C, D, E, F, G, H, I, J, K, L, M, N, O, P, Q, R, S, T, U, V, W, X, Y, Z

During this school year, children will begin to join some pairs of letters within a word.

They will be introduced to two main join types:

● Joins from the baseline, known as **diagonal joins**.

Letters which can come before diagonal joins: a, c, d, e, h, i, k, l, m, n, t, u.

diagonal join to short letter	diagonal join to an ascender	diagonal join to an anticlockwise letter
e.g. am, un jam, fun	e.g. at, th, ck bat, with, duck	e.g. ag, nd, if bag, bend, if

● Joins from the top of the letter or the cross bar, known as **horizontal joins**.

Letters which can come before horizontal joins: o, v, w.

horizontal join to a short letter	horizontal join to an ascender	horizontal join to an anticlockwise letter
e.g. on, wi pond, with	e.g. ot, oll, wh dot, doll, when	e.g. og, oc, oo frog, clock, look

Letters which are not joined from at this stage are known as **break letters** and include: b, f, g, j, p, q, r, s, x, y, z.

Variations in font throughout *Penpals*

FIVE DEVELOPMENTAL PHASES	SASSOON® CAMBRIDGE JOINER	*Penpals* Progression
1 GROSS AND FINE MOTOR SKILLS AND LETTER FORMATION	a	Each letter family is introduced with finger tracing letters incorporating the letter family artwork and a starting dot.
	b	Hollow letters with starting dots and arrows to show correct letter formation are also used for finger tracing.
	C	Solid letters with starting dots support letter formation.
	d	Independent writing with exit flicks is encouraged in preparation for joining.
2 BEGINNING TO JOIN	pen	Red is used for the focus join and joining letters to teach fluent formation.
3 SECURING THE JOINS	secure	Once all joins have been taught, all words are shown as joined for practice and consolidation.
4 PRACTISING SPEED AND FLUENCY	faster	Children are encouraged to develop an individual style for speed and legibility.
5 PRESENTATION SKILLS	individual print jokey	Further development of an individual style as well as presentation skills and techniques.

Penpals typesizes *

a a
Foundation 2/Primary 1
21mm/11.5mm

a a
Year 1/Primary 2
17mm/8mm

a
Year 2/Primary 3
5.5mm

a
Year 3/Primary 4
4mm

a
Year 4 onwards/
Primary 5 onwards
sloped, 4mm

* Letters in red are for finger tracing.
Letters in black are writing models.

1 Letter formation practice: long ladder family

Warm up

- 🖐 Children reach up high and bend down low. Use the vocabulary 'high' and 'low'.
- 🖐 Children stretch out their fingers. Can they stretch them wide and then make them narrow?

CD-ROM

Unit focus: identifying the long ladder family of letters; height of ascender and descender.
Phonic link: hearing initial phonemes.

Sky writing

Children copy the two patterns to review movements in the long ladder family. Say "Start at the top, come down." as children begin each movement.

Letter animation

Talk about the long ladder family mnemonic. Play the letter formation animation and say the patter. Children make the letter shape and say the patter.

Challenge words

Click on the toucan to see the challenge words. Children find the target letter pattern in the words.

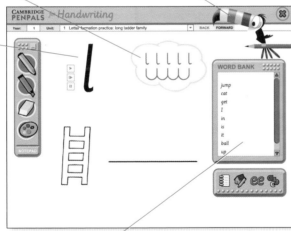

Word bank

Choose a word to discuss. Click on the word to make the long ladder letters grey. Model and discuss the letter formation.

Common errors

- incorrect relative heights of letters
- forgetting dots or putting huge dots on j and i
- letters leaning

Group work

Introduce the page

- Ask the children to look at the image in the middle of the page. Ask them: which letter family are we looking at? (long ladder family)

Skywriting patterns

- Sky write the patterns shown in the cloud. Use the following vocabulary: 'top', 'bottom', 'down', 'up', 'flick'.

Demonstrate the letter formations

- Trace over the long ladder in the middle, using the oral letter family patter (e.g. Make a long ladder: start at the top, come all the way down and flick).
- Demonstrate tracing the letters, always starting at the top. Note that t is shorter than l.
- Point out that j and y have a descender that curves to the left.
  Get Up and Go Ask the children to come up and point to letters which are short/tall/long.
  Show Me Children practise each letter in turn.

Independent work

Ask the children to turn to the lower case alphabet at the front of the Practice Book, and to find and finger trace the other letters in the long ladder family – i, t, u, j, y.

Watch while children trace the letters. Make sure they always start at the top. ❶

Make sure the children always write at least four of ❷ each letter (though they can do more if they like). Focus on the height of the letter and make sure letters that should sit on the line do.

Read the instruction. Help the children to read the words. ❸ They should recognise the high-frequency word *it*. Other high-frequency words the children could practise are *jump, just, last, little, time, too, took, take, tree, us, your*.

Encourage the children to practise the pattern in the bottom panel.

Practice Book page 2

Take away

① For additional letter formation practice use **PCM 1**.
② For additional practice use **Foundation 2 PCM 1 or 2** (long ladder letters and related patterns).

Big Book page 2

2 Letter formation practice: one-armed robot family

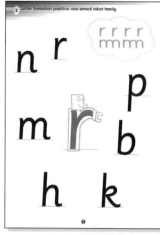

Big Book page 3

Warm up

- Children make one-armed robot shapes with their bodies.
- Children stretch and bend each finger of each hand in turn.

CD-ROM

Unit focus: identifying the one-armed robot family of letters.
Phonic link: hearing initial phonemes.

Sky writing

Children copy the two patterns to review movements in the one-armed robot family. Identify arches in one-armed robot letters.

Challenge word

Click on the toucan to see the challenge word. Children find the target letter pattern in the word.

Letter animation

Talk about the one-armed robot family mnemonic. Play the letter animation and say the patter. Children make the letter shape and say the patter.

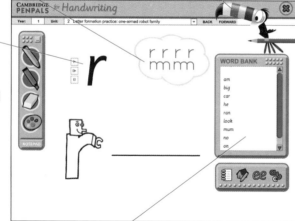

Word bank

Choose a word to discuss. Click on the word to make the one-armed robot letters grey. Model and discuss the letter formation.

Common errors

- not starting letters at the top
- incorrect position of the letters in relation to the baseline
- incorrect directionality of the one arm

Group work

Introduce the page

- Ask the children to look at the image in the middle of the page. Ask them: which letter family are we looking at? (one-armed robot family)

Skywriting patterns

- Sky write the patterns shown in the cloud. Emphasise the need to bounce up and over on both patterns.

Demonstrate the letter formations

- Demonstrate how to write the one-armed robot on the Big Book page, using the oral letter family patter (e.g. Make a robot: start at the top, come down and bounce back up and over).
- Demonstrate how to write each of the one-armed robot letters, reminding the children how to say the sound and the name of the letter.
  Get Up and Go Ask the children to identify which letters have an ascender (b, h and k) and which has a descender (p).
  Show Me Children practise each letter in turn.

Independent work

Ask the children to turn to the lower case alphabet at the front of the Practice Book, and to find and finger trace the other letters in the one-armed robot family – b, h, k, m, n, p.

Watch while the children trace the letters, making sure ❶ they start at the top each time. Make sure they notice those letters that sit on the line (with or without an ascender) and those that go below the line.

Children write the letters in their books. ❷

Help the children to read the words. Watch while the children ❸ write the words, ensuring orientation of all letters is correct and that letters start in the right place. On their second attempt, make sure the children use Look, Say, Cover, Write, Check.

Encourage the children to practise the pattern in the bottom panel. ❺

Can the children read these high-frequency words? Other high-frequency words they could practise are: *been, boy, but, ball, be, bed, how, home, house, man, new, not, now, ran, pull, put.*

Practice Book page 3

Take away

① For additional letter formation practice use **PCM 2**.

② For additional practice use **Foundation 2 PCM 3 or 4** (one-armed robot letters and related patterns).

3 Letter formation practice: curly caterpillar family

CD-ROM

Unit focus: identifying the curly caterpillar family of letters.
Phonic link: hearing initial phonemes.

Sky writing

Children copy the two patterns to review movements in the curly caterpillar family. Talk about the curve.

Challenge words

Click on the toucan to see the challenge words. Children find the target letter pattern in the words.

Letter animation

Talk about the curly caterpillar family mnemonic. Play the letter animation and say the patter. Children make the letter shape and say the patter.

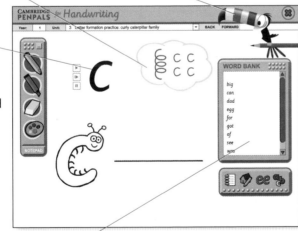

Word bank

Choose a word to discuss. Click on the word to make the curly caterpillar letters grey. Model and discuss the letter formation.

Common errors

- starting letters at 12 o'clock instead of 1 o'clock
- going round the letters the wrong way
- incorrect length of ascenders and descenders
- confusion of e and g

Group work

Introduce the page

- Ask the children to look at the image in the middle of the page. Ask them: which letter family are we looking at? (curly caterpillar family)

Skywriting patterns

- Sky write the patterns shown in the cloud, talking about 'curling over' and 'coming round'.

Demonstrate the letter formations

- Demonstrate how to write the curly caterpillar in the middle of the page, using the oral letter family patter (e.g. Make a caterpillar: start at the head, curve over the back and round).
  Get Up and Go Before you begin writing each of the letters, ask one of the children to come up and point to where the letter should begin.
- Demonstrate how to write the rest of the letters.
- Ask the children to tell you the sound and the name of each letter.
- Discuss which letters have a descender (f, g, q) and which have an ascender (d, f).
  Show Me Children practise each letter in turn.

Independent work

Ask the children to turn to the lower case alphabet at the front of the Practice Book, and to find and finger trace the other letters in the curly caterpillar family – a, d, e, f, g, o, q, s.

Watch while the children trace over the letters. ①
Make sure they start each letter in the right place.

Children write the letters in their books. ②

Help the children to read all the words before they write them.

Encourage the children to practise the pattern in the bottom panel.

Ask the children to read all these high-frequency words before they attempt to write them. Check on letter formation each time. Make sure the children use Look, Say, Cover, Write, Check. Other high-frequency words they could practise are: *an, as, call, came, can't, did, do, dig, door, down, first, girl, good, got, or, our, out, over, so, some, seen, saw.*

Take away

① For additional letter formation practice use **PCM 3**.

② For additional practice use **Foundation 2 PCM 5 or 6** (curly caterpillar letters and related patterns).

Big Book page 4

Practice Book page 4

Warm up

 Children make zig-zag shapes, bending at different parts of their body (elbows, knees).

Children make zig-zag shapes with their hands and fingers.

CD-ROM

Unit focus: identifying the zig-zag monster family.
Phonic link: hearing initial and final phonemes.

Sky writing

Children copy the two patterns to review movements in the zig-zag monster family. Talk about the straight lines, sharp points and slopes.

Letter animation

Talk about the zig-zag monster family mnemonic. Play the letter animation and say the patter. Children make the letter shape and say the patter.

Challenge word

Click on the toucan to see the challenge word. Children find the target letter pattern in the word.

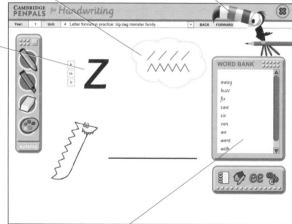

Word bank

Choose a word to discuss. Click on the word to make the zig-zag monster letters grey. Model and discuss the letter formation.

Common errors

- reversal of z
- exaggeration of the middle point of w
- incorrect formation of x

Group work

Introduce the page

- Ask the children to look at the image at the top of the page. Ask them: which letter family are we looking at? (zig-zag monster family)

Skywriting patterns

- Sky write the patterns shown in the cloud, emphasising the sharp points and the diagonal lines.

Demonstrate the letter formations

- Demonstrate how to write the letter z at the top of the page, using the oral letter family patter (e.g. Make a monster: start by going straight across to the head, then go down the back and then straight across again).

Big Book page 5

- Demonstrate how to form the other letters, paying particular attention to x.
  Get Up and Go Can the children tell you where to start writing each letter?
- Ask children to name the letters and say which sound they make.
- Do the children recognise the pictures?
  Get Up and Go Invite the children to trace lines across the page to join each letter to the space where it should appear.
- Demonstrate writing each letter in the right space, reminding children where to start.
  Show Me Children practise each letter in turn.

Independent work

Ask the children to turn to the lower case alphabet at the front of the Practice Book, and to find and finger trace the other letters in the zig-zag monster family – v, w, x.

Watch while the children trace the letters. Make sure ❶ they start each letter in the correct place.

Children write the letter patterns in their books. ❷

Ask the children if they recognise the pictures. Read the ❸ words together and then watch while the children write the words, making sure their letter formation is correct.

Encourage the children to practise the pattern in the bottom panel.

Practice Book page 5

❺

❹

Ask the children to read and then write these high-frequency words. Make sure the children use Look, Say, Cover, Write, Check. Other high-frequency words they could practise are: *how, live, love, new, now, next, over, saw, very, we, went, want, water, way, were, what, when, who, will, with, would.*

Take away

① For additional letter formation practice use **PCM 4**.

② For additional practice use **Foundation 2 PCM 7 or 8** (zig-zag letters and related patterns).

Warm up

🖑 Children stretch up high and bend down low. Emphasise high/low, tall/short, big/little.

🖑 Children stretch their fingers out as tall as they can and then make them as short as possible.

CD-ROM

Unit focus: letter formation practice – all families.
Phonic link: CVC words with medial short vowel **i**.

Sky writing

Children copy the two patterns to review movements in the formation of *i*. Talk about the straight lines, exit flicks and dots.

Challenge words

Click on the toucan to see the challenge words. Children find the target letter pattern in the words. They could also find the letter pattern in a word represented by the artwork.

Letter animation

The letter animation allows the review of the letter formation for *i*. Talk about the letter name and sound. Talk about words that feature the letter *i*.

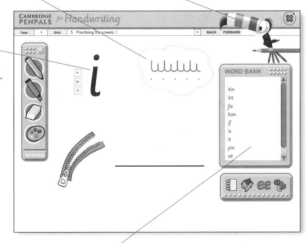

Word bank

Choose a word to discuss. Click on the word to make the *i* grey for modelling. Discuss the letter formation and read the word.

Common errors

- dot on *i* too large
- ascenders and descenders too long or too short

Group work

Introduce the page

- Encourage the children to talk about the page before you begin. Talk about the sound in the middle of all the words (short vowel phoneme **i**).
- Which letter family does *i* belong to? (long ladder family)

Skywriting patterns

- Sky write the patterns shown in the cloud.

Demonstrate the letter formations

- Demonstrate tracing and writing the word *big*, emphasising that the *b* has an ascender and is about twice the height of the *i*. The *g* sits on the line but its descender goes beneath the line and curves to the left. It should be about as long as the *b* is tall.
- Model tracing over the *i* in the words *lid* and *zip*. Highlight the ascender on the letter *d* and the descender on the letter *p*. Model writing the whole words under the small lid and zip pictures.
- Model tracing over the *i* in the word *six*. Point out that all the letters are the same size (but the dot on the *i* goes up high). Again, demonstrate how to write the word under the small picture of a six.
Get Up and Go Can the children point to the matching pictures? There is a big and a little version of each picture. Ask the children to draw a line from each picture to the word *big* or *little* as appropriate.
Show Me Ask the children to write the word *big*. Repeat for the other words.

Independent work

Watch while the children finger trace the letters and say ❶ the sound. Ask them: which letters have ascenders (*t*) and which have descenders (*p* and *g*)?

Children write the letters in their books. ❷

Before children write the words, read them together, using ❸ the picture cues. In which word are the letters all the same size? (*win*) Which words have ascenders (*tin* and *dig*) and which have descenders? (*dig* and *pip*)

Encourage the children to practise the pattern in the bottom panel.

Can the children Look, Say, Cover, Write and Check these high-frequency words? Another high-frequency word they could practise is *him*.

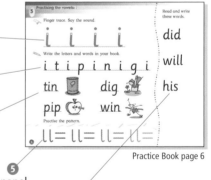

Practice Book page 6

Take away

① For additional letter formation practice use **PCM 5**.
② For additional practice use **all Foundation 2 PCMs, especially PCMs 1 and 2** (long ladder letters and related patterns).

Big Book page 6

6 Practising the vowels: u

Warm up

- Children draw big hoops in the air, then little hoops. They draw them slowly and then fast.
- Children make little hoops by touching each finger in turn to their thumb.

CD-ROM

Unit focus: letter formation practice – all letter families.
Phonic link: CVC words with medial short vowel **u**.

Sky writing

Children copy the two patterns to review movements in the formation of u. Talk about the size of the exit flick and the importance of flow.

Letter animation

The letter animation allows the review of the letter formation for u. Talk about the letter name and sound. Talk about words that feature the letter u.

Challenge word

Click on the toucan to see the challenge word. Children find the target letter pattern in the word. They could also find the letter pattern in a word represented by the artwork.

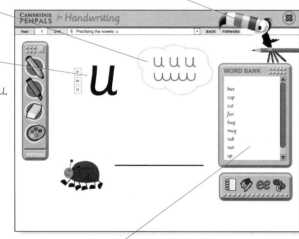

Word bank

Choose a word to discuss. Click on the word to make the u grey for modelling. Discuss the letter formation and read the word.

Common errors

- ascenders and descenders too long or too short
- letters not sitting on the line or descenders not going below the line

bug

Group work

Introduce the page

- Encourage the children to talk about the page before you begin.
- Read the speech bubbles together. Ask the children: which sound is in the middle of all these words? (short vowel phoneme **u**)
- Which letter family does u belong to? (long ladder family)

Skywriting patterns

- Sky write the patterns shown in the cloud.

Demonstrate the letter formations

- Point to each speech bubble in turn and agree which letter is missing in each word. Fill in the us.
- Trace over *bug* and discuss the ascender on the b and the descender on the g.
- Complete and trace the words *nut* and *mud*, talking through the letter formation each time.
  Get Up and Go Ask children to put a tick beside the pictures of things the chicken would like to eat and a cross beside the others.
  Show Me Children write each word in turn.

Big Book page 7

Independent work

Watch while the children finger trace the letters and say ① the sound. Ask them: which letters have ascenders (h) and which have descenders (g)?

Children write the letters in their books. ②

Before children write the words, read them together, using ③ the picture cues. Which words have letters that are all the same size? (*sun* and *mum*) Which have letters with ascenders (*hut*) and descenders? (*jug*)

Encourage the children to practise the pattern in the bottom panel.

Practice Book page 7

Can the children Look, Say, Cover, Write and Check these high-frequency words? Another high-frequency word they could practise is *pull*.

Take away

① For additional letter formation practice use **PCM 6**.
② For additional practice use **all Foundation 2 PCMs, especially PCMs 1 and 2** (long ladder letters and related patterns).

Warm up

- Children work in pairs and clap their hands against their partner's hands. They then clap normally themselves. Can they make a rhythm using these different kinds of clap?
- Children stretch their hands as wide as they can, then relax them. Then they curl their hands up tight, and then relax them.

 **CD-ROM**

Unit focus: letter formation practice – all letter families.
Phonic link: CVC words with medial short vowel **a**.

Sky writing

Children copy the two patterns to review movements in the formation of *a*. Talk about the direction of the curves and the importance of flow.

Letter animation

The letter animation allows the review of the letter formation for *a*. Talk about the letter name and sound. Talk about words that feature the letter *a*.

Challenge word

Click on the toucan to see the challenge word. Children find the target letter pattern in the word. They could also find the letter pattern in a word represented by the artwork.

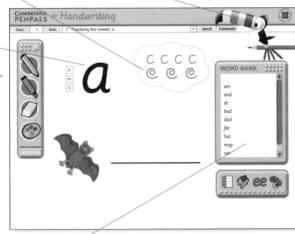

Word bank

Choose a word to discuss. Click on the word to make the *a* grey for modelling. Discuss the letter formation and read the word.

Common errors

- starting *a* at the 12 o'clock position instead of at 1 o'clock
- overlapping at the top or failing to close the letter

Group work

Introduce the page

- Encourage the children to talk about the page before you begin.
- Can the children identify the pictures? Ask them: which sound is in the middle of all these words? (short vowel phoneme **a**)

Skywriting patterns

- Sky write the patterns shown in the cloud, talking about the direction of the curves (anticlockwise).

Demonstrate the letter formations

- Model tracing over the *a* in *can* and *cat*.
- Point to each of the pictures in turn. Ask the children which letter we need to complete each word. Demonstrate writing the letters. **Show Me** When you have demonstrated each of the words, children write them.
  Get Up and Go Can the children count the *a*s on the page?
- Can children think of any other words with the medial vowel sound **a**? Demonstrate how to write them.

Big Book page 8

Independent work

Watch while the children trace over the letters. ❶ Make sure they start in the right place and that all the letters rest on the line.

Children write the letters in their books. ❷

Do the children recognise the pictures? Ask them to ❸ read the words. Watch as they write the words, making sure that the letters are the correct height. Make sure the children use Look, Say, Cover, Write, Check.

Encourage the children to practise the pattern in the bottom panel.

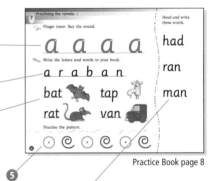

Practice Book page 8

Read these high-frequency words with the children. Other high-frequency words they could practise are *has, cat, can*.

Take away

① For additional letter formation practice use **PCM 7**.
② For additional practice use **all Foundation 2 PCMs, especially PCMs 5 and 6** (curly caterpillar letters and related patterns).

8 Practising the vowels: o

Warm up

- Children make big spiral shapes in the air using both their arms at the same time.
- Children interlock their fingers and then straighten them, one pair at a time.

CD-ROM

Unit focus: letter formation practice – all letter families.
Phonic link: CVC words with medial short vowel **o**.

Sky writing

Children copy the two patterns to review movements in the formation of o. Talk about the direction and the importance of ending where you began.

Challenge word

Click on the toucan to see the challenge word. Children find the target letter pattern in the word. They could also find the letter pattern in a word represented by the artwork.

Letter animation

The letter animation allows the review of the letter formation for o. Talk about the letter name and sound. Talk about words that feature the letter o.

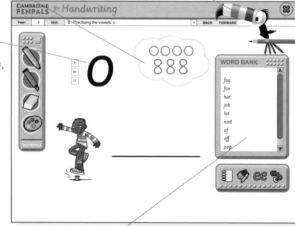

Word bank

Choose a word to discuss. Click on the word to make the o grey for modelling. Discuss the letter formation and read the word.

Common errors

- clockwise rather than anticlockwise movement to form the o
- ascenders and descenders too long or too short

hop top

Group work

Introduce the page

- Read the text on the Big Book page together. Tell the children that each line is like a little rhyme and that the first and last words should rhyme. Can they work out the missing word each time? (*hop on a top; jog on a log; dot on a pot*)
- Ask the children: which letter family does o belong to? (curly caterpillar family)

Skywriting patterns

- Sky write the patterns shown in the cloud.

Demonstrate the letter formations

- Demonstrate, by tracing over, how to write the first word on each line. As you do so, remind children of the anticlockwise movement needed to make the o.
- Discuss which letters are short and which have an ascender or a descender.
- Write the missing words yourself, if possible asking children to spell the words aloud.
  Get Up and Go Can the children identify the other words on the page that contain an o? (*on, you*)
  Show Me Children write the missing word from each line.

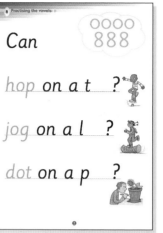

Big Book page 9

Independent work

Watch while the children finger trace the letters and say the sound. Ask them to tell you which letters have ascenders (d) and which have descenders (p and g).

Children write the letters in their books.

Read the words together, using the picture cues. Ask children which words have letters with ascenders (*box, dog* and *cot*) and descenders (*mop*).

Encourage the children to practise the pattern in the bottom panel. Make sure they start the circle at the 1 o'clock position.

Can the children Look, Say, Cover, Write and Check these high-frequency words?

Practice Book page 9

Take away

① For additional letter formation practice use **PCM 8**.
② For additional practice use **all Foundation 2 PCMs, especially PCMs 5 and 6** (curly caterpillar letters and related patterns).

Warm up

👆 Children make big spiral movements. Some of the spirals should travel upwards, others down or to the left.

👆 Children put the heels of their hands together and 'clap' each pair of fingers in turn. Finish off by giving the hands a good shake.

CD-ROM

Unit focus: letter formation practice – all letter families.
Phonic link: CVC words with medial short vowel **e**.

Sky writing

Children copy the two patterns to review the movements in the formation of *e*. Talk about the importance of keeping the flow.

Challenge words

Click on the toucan to see the challenge words. Children find the target letter pattern in the words. They could also find the letter pattern in a word represented by the artwork.

Letter animation

The letter animation allows the review of the letter formation for *e*. Talk about the letter name and sound. Talk about words that feature the letter *e*.

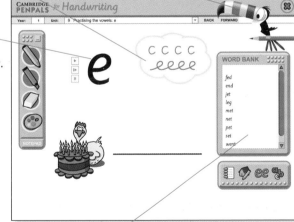

Word bank

Choose a word to discuss. Click on the word to make the *e* grey for modelling. Discuss the letter formation and read the word.

Common errors

- *e* too large
- ascenders and descenders too long or too short

Group work

Introduce the page

- Read the questions on the Big Book page together.
- Ask the children: which letter family does *e* belong to? (curly caterpillar family)

Skywriting patterns

- Sky write the patterns shown in the cloud, emphasising the anticlockwise movement.

Demonstrate the letter formations

- Model how to write the words *yes* and *no* by tracing over them.
- Read the questions again, this time demonstrating tracing over the *e* in each of the words.
  Get Up and Go Ask children to come out and point to the correct answer for each question.
  Show Me Children write *yes* and *no*.
- Ask each of the children to choose a word with medial vowel sound **e** and to write it down secretly. Can they give clues so that their partner can guess the word? (e.g. It starts with *w* and ends with *b*.)

Big Book page 10

Independent work

Watch while the children finger trace the letters and say ① the sound. Ask them to tell you which letters have ascenders and which have descenders.

Children write the letters in their books. ②

Read the words together, using the picture cues. ③ Children write the words. In which word are the letters all the same size? (*men*) Which words have letters with ascenders (*ten*) or descenders? (*pegs*)

Encourage the children to practise the pattern in the bottom panel.

Can the children Look, Say, Cover, Write and Check these high-frequency words?

Practice Book page 10

Take away

① For additional letter formation practice use **PCM 9**.
② For additional practice use **all Foundation 2 PCMs, especially PCMs 5 and 6** (curly caterpillar letters and related patterns).

10 Letter formation practice: capital letters

Warm up

✋ Children make big spiky movements with their whole arms.

✋ Children make little spiky movements (like fireworks exploding) with their hands, wrists and fingers.

CD-ROM

Unit focus: letter formation practice – capitals.

Phonic links: knowing which sound is represented by each capital letter; to practise and secure alphabetic letter knowledge and alphabetical order.

Sky writing

Children copy the two patterns to review movements in the formation of capital letters. Talk about the importance of straight lines.

Challenge word

Click on the toucan to see the challenge word. Children show the lower case equivalent of each of its letters. They could also identify the onomatopoeic words represented in the artwork.

Phrase animation

The phrase animation allows the review of the capital letter formations. Talk about the letter names and sounds. Talk about names in the class that begin with these capitals.

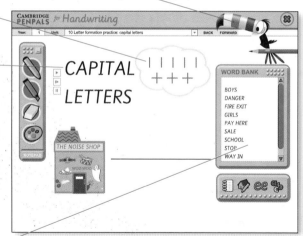

Word bank

Choose a word or phrase to discuss. Click on a word or phrase to make the letters grey for modelling. Discuss the letter formation and read the word or phrase.

Common errors

- letters varying in size
- letters not sitting on the line (though the stroke on Q may dip slightly beneath the line)

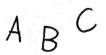

Group work

Introduce the page

- Talk about the page together, reading all the text.
- Discuss the representation of each noise using capital letters. Why might you use capital letters rather than lower case ones?
- Can the children tell you which sound each of these capital letters represents?
- What other uses of capital letters can the children see on the page? (shop name, 'open' notice) Is it normal to write a whole word in capital letters? When do you use a capital letter?
- Ask the children: what other things that make noises might be sold in The Noise Shop?

Big Book page 11

Skywriting patterns

- Sky write the patterns shown in the cloud.

Demonstrate the letter formations

- Model how to write the words by tracing over them, talking through the letter formations as you do so.
  Show Me Ask each of the children to write their name. Have they used a capital letter only at the beginning? Ask the children to write the noise of something they could sell in the shop. They should use capital letters throughout the word to represent the noise.

Independent work

Watch while the children write the alphabet in capital ❶ letters. All the letters should start at the top and be roughly the same size. They should all sit on the line.

Encourage the children to practise the pattern in the ❸ bottom panel.

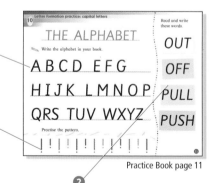
Practice Book page 11

Can the children Look, Say, Cover, Write and Check these high-frequency words?

Take away

① For additional letter formation practice use **PCM 10**.

② For additional practice use **Foundation 2 PCMs 1–8** (all letter families, plus related patterns).

11 Introducing diagonal join to ascender: joining *at*, *all*

Warm up

- 👋 Children make themselves tall and short, stretching up high and crouching down low.
- 👋 Children stretch their fingers out and then curl them up tight.

CD-ROM

Unit focus: joining *at* and *all*.
Phonic link: CVC words ending in **ll**.

Sky writing

Children copy the two patterns to introduce the diagonal join to ascender. Talk about the importance of straight lines.

Challenge word

Click on the toucan to see the challenge word. Children find the target letter pattern in the word. They could also find the letter pattern in a word represented by the artwork.

Join animations

The letter patterns demonstrate the diagonal join to ascender. Talk about the letter patterns and the upward sweep of the join.

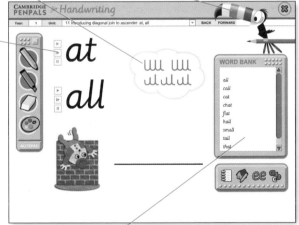

Word bank

Choose a word to discuss. Click on the word to make the diagonal to ascender join grey. Model and discuss the join movement.

Common errors

- the t and the l same height as the a
- making a jerky movement rather than a fluent one, because the hand is tense (If this is the case, children should go back to the warm up.) *at all*

Group work

Introduce the page

- Identify the letter patterns at the top of the page.
- Ask children to point to the *at* and *all* in the words, and to speculate about the endings for the words with blanks.

Skywriting patterns

- Sky write the patterns shown in the cloud. As you do so, emphasise the fluid movement.

Demonstrate the join

- Introduce the word *join*. Explain that it means writing a sequence of two or more letters without taking your pencil off the page. This helps you to write quickly and more easily.
- Demonstrate by tracing over *at* at the top of the page. As you finish forming the *a* tell the children you are keeping the pencil on the page and going right up to the top of the *t* and then forming the *t* as usual.
- Demonstrate tracing over the join again, before asking the children to sky write it.
  Show Me Can the children write *at*? Check that the join is fluent and that they don't add the cross bar to the *t* until the join is complete. Repeat for the letter pattern *all*.
- Tracing over the grey letters in the words next to the picture, demonstrate how to write them.
  Show Me Children copy the words.
- Ask the children: which letter patterns do we need to complete the other words? Model writing them.

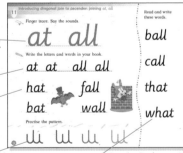

Big Book page 12

Independent work

Watch while the children finger trace the letters and say ① the sounds. Make sure they keep their fingers on the page while they trace each of the letter patterns.

Children write the letter patterns in their books. ②

Read the words together, using the picture cues. ③ Children then copy each word. Check that the children do not lift their pencil before the join is complete.

Children practise the pattern. ④

Can the children Look, Say, Cover, Write and Check these high-frequency words? ⑤

Practice Book page 12

Take away

For additional practice of this join use **PCM 11**.

12 Practising diagonal join to ascender: joining *th*

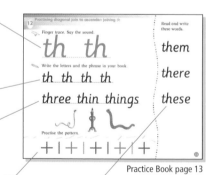

> *Dear Gran,*
>
> *Thank you for the thick gloves. They will keep my thumbs warm with all that wool.*
>
> *Love from*
>
> *Gareth*

Warm up

 Children draw patterns of loops in the sky, trying to achieve three different heights: tall loops, medium-sized loops and short loops.

Children sing the finger rhyme Tommy Thumb (see **Foundation 1 CD**, track 18; **Teacher's Book**, page 46).

CD-ROM

Unit focus: joining *th*.

Phonic link: th consonant digraph.

Sky writing

Children copy the two patterns to practise the diagonal join to ascender. Talk about the importance of the flow.

Challenge word

Click on the toucan to see the challenge word. Children find the target letter pattern in the word. They could also find the letter pattern in a word represented by the artwork.

Join animation

The letter pattern demonstrates the diagonal join to ascender. Talk about the letter pattern and the upward sweep of the join.

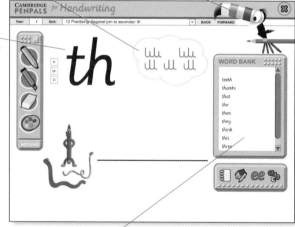

Word bank

Choose a word to discuss. Click on the word to make the diagonal to ascender join grey. Model and discuss the join movement.

Common errors

- making the *t* and the *h* the same size (the *t* should be shorter)
- putting the cross bar on the *t* before finishing the join
- forgetting the exit flick on the *h*

Group work

Introduce the page

- Identify the letter pattern at the top of the page.
- Read the letter to Gran aloud with the children.
- Re-read it, asking children to raise their hands when they hear a **th** sound.

Skywriting patterns

- Sky write the patterns shown in the cloud. Emphasise the fluid movement and the differences in height, even if these are only very slight.

Demonstrate the join

- Demonstrate how to join the *th* at the top of the page.
- Remind the children that the *t* is shorter than the *h*.
- Point out how you cross the *t* after you have done the join.

  Get Up and Go Invite children to circle all the *th* patterns they can identify in the text. Remind them to look at the end as well as at the beginning of words. Model tracing over the grey *th*s. Point out to children that capital letters never join.

  Show Me Children write the *th* pattern.

Independent work

Watch while the children finger trace the letters and say the sound. Make sure they keep their fingers on the page while they trace the letter pattern and only cross the *t* after the join has been completed. Ask the children to finger trace the letter pattern several times.

Children write the letter pattern in their books.

Read the phrase together, using the picture cues. Children write the phrase in their books. (They can do this more than once if there is time and space.) Check that the children do not lift their pencil before the join is complete.

Children practise the pattern.

Can the children Look, Say, Cover, Write and Check these high-frequency words? Other high-frequency words they could practise are: *the, they, this, than, that, their, then.*

Take away

For additional practice of this join use **PCM 12**.

Warm up

- Children pretend to be trains and say 'ch, ch, ch' while making train-like arm movements.
- Children show you their fingers, knuckles, wrists, palms, thumbs. They trace the lines on their palms and then give their hands a shake.

CD-ROM

Unit focus: joining *ch*.
Phonic link: **ch** consonant digraph.

Sky writing

Children copy the two patterns to practise the diagonal join to ascender. Talk about the importance of the flow.

Join animation

The letter pattern demonstrates the diagonal join to ascender. Talk about the letter pattern and the upward sweep of the join.

Challenge word

Click on the toucan to see the challenge word. Children find the target letter pattern in the word. They could also find the letter pattern in a word represented by the artwork.

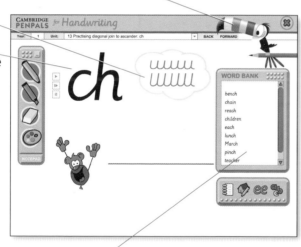

Word bank

Choose a word to discuss. Click on the word to make the diagonal to ascender join grey. Model and discuss the join movement.

Common errors

- letters too close together, so that the c looks like a d
- forgetting the exit flick on the h
- not bouncing back up on the h or bouncing up too high

Group work

Introduce the page

- Identify the letter pattern at the top of the page and read the words aloud with the children.

Skywriting patterns

- Sky write the patterns shown in the cloud, emphasising the fluid movement.

Demonstrate the join

- Demonstrate how to join the *ch* at the top of the page.
- Emphasise the fluidity of the movement and the relative height of each letter.
- Remind children that the pencil shouldn't leave the paper when joining.
- Model tracing over the *ch*s in the phrase *cheeky chimp*.
  Show Me Children write the *ch* pattern.
- Ask children to identify the last activity in the picture (*chop*). Model tracing over the *ch*s again.

Big Book page 14

Independent work

Watch while the children finger trace the letters and say **①** the sound. Make sure they keep their fingers on the page while they trace the letter pattern. Ask the children to finger trace the letter pattern several times.

Children write the letter pattern in their books. **②**

Read the phrase together, using the picture cue. Children **③** copy the phrase into their books. (They can do this more than once if there is time and space.) Check that the children do not lift their pencil before the join is complete. **⑤**

Children practise the pattern.

Can the children Look, Say, Cover, Write and Check these words? **④**

Practice Book page 14

Take away

For additional practice of this join use **PCM 13**.

Warm up

- Children clap their hands above their heads, to the right, down beside their knees, and so on.
- Children put the heels of their hands together and 'clap' each pair of fingers in turn.

 **CD-ROM**

Unit focus: joining *cl*.
Phonic link: consonant cluster **cl**.

Sky writing

Children copy the two patterns to practise the letter flow of *c* to *l*: diagonal join to ascender. Emphasise the flow of the movement and the relative height of each letter.

Challenge word

Click on the toucan to see the challenge word. Children find the target letter pattern in the word. They could also find the letter pattern in a word represented by the artwork.

Join animation

The letter pattern demonstrates the diagonal join to ascender. Talk about the letter pattern and the upward sweep of the join.

Word bank

Choose a word to discuss. Click on the word to make the diagonal to ascender join grey. Model and discuss the join movement.

Common errors

- letters too close together, so that the *c* looks like a *d*
- forgetting the exit flick on the *l*
- incorrect relative heights of letters

Group work

Introduce the page

- Read the letter pattern at the top of the page and identify the various elements of the picture.

Skywriting patterns

- Sky write the patterns shown in the cloud. As you do so, emphasise the fluid movement between the shapes.

Demonstrate the join

- Demonstrate how to join the *cl* at the top of the page.
- Emphasise the fluidity of the movement and the relative height of each letter.
- Remind the children that their pencil shouldn't leave the paper while they are joining letters.
  Get Up and Go Ask children to point to the *cl* in the phrase *clever clown*. Can the children find the hidden *cl*s in the picture?
- Model writing *cl* in the gaps to make the words *clap clap*.
  Show Me Children practise writing *cl*.

Big Book page 15

Independent work

Watch while the children finger trace the letters and say **1** the sound. Make sure they keep their fingers on the page while they trace the letter pattern. Ask the children to finger trace the letter pattern several times.

Children write the letter pattern in their books. **2**

Read the phrase together, using the picture cue. **3** Children copy the phrase into their books. (They can do this more than once if there is time and space.) Check that the children do not lift their pencil before the join is complete.

Children practise the pattern. **5**

Can the children Look, Say, Cover, Write and Check these words? **4**

Practice Book page 15

Take away

For additional practice of this join use **PCM 14**.

15 Introducing diagonal join, no ascender: joining *in*, *im*

Warm up

- Children stretch up high then curl into a ball and jump up.
- Children count from one to ten on their fingers, beginning with fists and stretching out one finger at a time.

CD-ROM

Unit focus: joining *in* and *im*.
Phonic link: segmenting and blending CVC words.

Sky writing

Children copy the two patterns to introduce the diagonal join, no ascender. Emphasise that the ascenders in the second pattern are the same height.

Challenge word

Click on the toucan to see the challenge word. Children find the target letter pattern in the word. They could also find the letter pattern in a word represented by the artwork.

Join animations

The letter patterns demonstrate the diagonal join, no ascender. Talk about the letter patterns and the equal height of the letters.

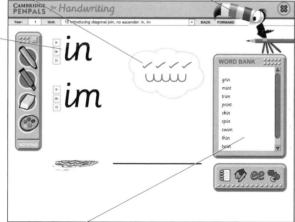

Word bank

Choose a word to discuss. Click on the word to make the diagonal join, no ascender, grey. Model and discuss the join movement.

Common errors

- incorrect orientation of letters
- not starting letters at the top
- lifting the pencil to dot the *i* before completing the join

Group work

Introduce the page
- Read the letter patterns and identify the pictures.

Skywriting patterns
- Introduce the patterns with sky writing.

Demonstrate the join
- Demonstrate writing the letter pattern *in*.
- Emphasise that the letters are the same height.
  Get Up and Go Ask children to point out the objects that end with *in*.
- Model writing *in* by tracing over and finishing the words *bin*, *pin*, *tin* and *fin*.
  Show Me Children write the letter pattern *in*.
- Repeat with *im* (and the word *dim*).

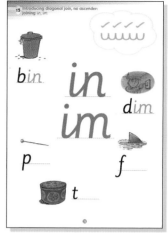

Big Book page 16

Independent work

Watch while the children finger trace the letters and say the sounds. Make sure they complete the join before dotting the *i*. Ask the children to finger trace each letter pattern several times. ❶

Children write the letter patterns in their books. ❷

Read the words together, using the picture cues. Children copy the words into their books. (They can do this more than once if there is time and space.) Check that the children do not lift their pencil before the join is complete. ❺

Children practise the pattern. ❹

Can the children Look, Say, Cover, Write and Check these high-frequency words?

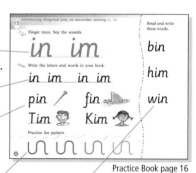

Practice Book page 16

Take away

For additional practice of this join use **PCM 15**.

16 Practising diagonal join, no ascender: joining *cr*, *tr*, *dr*

Warm up

✋ Children pretend to play different musical instruments, including drum, guitar, recorder and violin.

✋ Children put the heels of their hands together and 'clap' each pair of fingers in turn. Finish off by giving the hands a good shake.

CD-ROM

Unit focus: joining *cr*, *tr*, *dr*.
Phonic link: initial consonant clusters **cr**, **tr**, **dr**.

Sky writing

Children copy the two patterns to practise the diagonal join, no ascender. Emphasise the relative heights of the letters in the second pattern.

Challenge word

Click on the toucan to see the challenge word. Children find the target letter pattern in the word. They could also find the letter pattern in a word represented by the artwork.

Join animations

The letter patterns demonstrate the diagonal join, no ascender. Talk about the letter patterns and the relative heights of the letters.

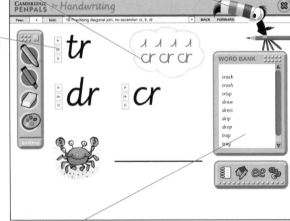

Word bank

Choose a word to discuss. Click on the word to make the diagonal join, no ascender, grey. Model and discuss the join movement.

Common errors

- incorrect relative height of letters
- inadequately formed joins

Group work

Introduce the page

- Read the letter patterns and identify the pictures.

Skywriting patterns

- Sky write the patterns shown in the cloud. As you do so, emphasise the fluid movement between the shapes.

Demonstrate the join

- Demonstrate the letter patterns. Emphasise the fluidity of the movement and the relative height of each letter. Remind the children that their pencil shouldn't leave the paper while they are joining letters. Ask them to remind you when they should cross the *t* (when the join is complete).

- Can the children identify which letter pattern is needed to complete each word? Demonstrate writing the appropriate letter pattern each time. **Show Me** As you write each word, the children copy it.

- Can the children suggest any other words beginning with any of these letter patterns? Write them up for the class to copy.

Big Book page 17

Independent work

Watch while the children finger trace the letters and say ① the sounds. Make sure they keep their fingers on the page while they trace each of the letter patterns, and that they don't cross the *t* until the join is complete. Ask the children to finger trace each letter pattern several times.

Children write the letter patterns in their books. ②

Read the words together, using the picture cues. ③ Children copy the words in their books. Ask the children to tell you which letters they are joining in each word.

Children practise the pattern. ⑤

Can the children Look, Say, Cover, Write and Check these words? ④

Practice Book page 17

Take away

For additional practice of this join use **PCM 16**.

Warm up

✋ Children hop on the spot. Can they hop five times on one foot and then five times on the other?

✋ Children 'hop' on the palm of their left hand with each of the fingers of their right hand in turn. Then repeat, swapping the hands over.

CD-ROM

Unit focus: joining *lp*, *mp*.
Phonic link: final consonant clusters **lp**, **mp**.

Sky writing

Children copy the two patterns to practise the diagonal join, no ascender. Emphasise the swing up to join and then the downward stroke.

Challenge word

Click on the toucan to see the challenge word. Children find the target letter pattern in the word. They could also find the letter pattern in a word represented by the artwork.

Join animations

The letter patterns demonstrate the diagonal join, no ascender. Talk about the letter patterns, the swing up of the join and the downward movement to form the descender of the *p*.

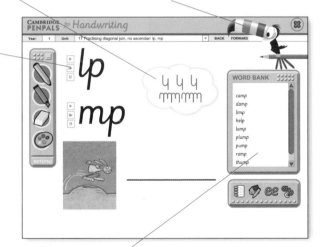

Word bank

Choose a word to discuss. Click on the word to make the diagonal join, no ascender, grey. Model and discuss the join movement.

Common errors

- incorrect relative height of letters
- *p* not sitting on the line, with descender not falling below it

Group work

Introduce the page

- Talk through the cartoon-strip. Can the children retell the story?

Skywriting patterns

- Sky write the patterns shown in the cloud. As you do so, emphasise the fluid movement between the shapes and the way that some shapes start high, while others end low.

Demonstrate the join

- Read the letter patterns and demonstrate the joins.
- Emphasise the fluidity of the movement and the relative height of each letter. Remind the children that their pencil shouldn't leave the paper while they are joining letters.
- Can the children identify which letter pattern is needed to complete each word? Demonstrate writing the letter pattern each time.
  Show Me As you demonstrate each word, the children write it.
- Can the children suggest any other words ending with either of these letter patterns? (e.g. *camp*, *lamp*, *imp*; *yelp*, *gulp*) Write them up for the children to copy.

Big Book page 18

Independent work

Watch while the children finger trace the letters and say ❶ the sounds. Make sure they keep their fingers on the page while they trace each of the letter patterns. Ask the children to finger trace each letter pattern several times.

Children write the letter patterns in their books. ❷

Read the words together, using the picture cues. ❸ Children write the words in their books. Ask the children to tell you which letters they are joining in each word.

Encourage children to practise the pattern in the bottom panel.

Can the children Look, Say, Cover, Write and Check these high-frequency words?

Practice Book page 18

Take away

For additional practice of this join use **PCM 17**.

Big Book page 19

Warm up

🖐 Children mime a digging action, then a raking action (towards the body), then a sweeping action (away from the body).

🖐 Children close all the fingers of one hand into a fist, then very slowly make their hands 'grow' until they are fully stretched. Repeat with the other hand.

CD-ROM

Unit focus: joining *id, ig*.
Phonic link: reading and writing CVC words.

Sky writing

Children copy the two patterns to practise the diagonal join, no ascender, to an anticlockwise letter. Emphasise the crossing of the midpoint of the figure of 8.

Join animations

The letter patterns demonstrate the diagonal join, no ascender, to an anticlockwise letter. Talk about the letter patterns: the curve up and over to make the join, then the retrace back in order to finish the second letter.

Challenge word

Click on the toucan to see the challenge word. Children find the target letter pattern in the word. They could also find the letter pattern in a word represented by the artwork.

Word bank

Choose a word to discuss. Click on the word to make the diagonal join, no ascender, to an anticlockwise letter grey. Model and discuss the join movement.

Common errors

- not reversing
- descender too long
- diagonal join too steep

Group work

Introduce the page

- Identify the letter patterns and the pictures.

Skywriting patterns

- Sky write the patterns shown in the cloud. As you do so, emphasise the fluid movement.

Demonstrate the join

- Read the letter patterns and demonstrate the joins.
- Emphasise the fluidity of the movement and the relative height of each letter. Remind the children that their pencil shouldn't leave the paper while they are joining letters.
- Help the children to see how you need to curve up and over to make the join, then stop and trace back over the line in the opposite (anticlockwise) direction before finishing the second letter.
- Can the children identify which letter pattern is needed to complete each word? Demonstrate writing the appropriate letter pattern each time.
  Show Me As you demonstrate each word, the children write it.

Independent work

Watch while the children finger trace the letters and say ➊ the sounds. Make sure they keep their fingers on the page while they trace each of the letter patterns. Ask them to finger trace each letter pattern several times.

Children write the letter patterns in their books. ➋

Read the words together, using the picture cues. ➌ Children write the words in their books. Ask the children to tell you which letters they are joining in each word. ➎

Encourage the children to practise the pattern in the bottom panel. ➍

Can the children Look, Say, Cover, Write and Check these words?

Practice Book page 19

Take away

For additional practice of this join use **PCM 18**.

Warm up

🖐 Children 'sky draw' a face and use both hands to add hair. The hair can be spiky, curly, long, short, straight, etc.

🖐 Children draw rainbow shapes on each other's backs. The rainbows should go from left to right and the children should use different fingers to draw them.

CD-ROM

Unit focus: joining *nd, ld*.
Phonic link: final consonant clusters.

Sky writing

Children copy the two patterns to practise the diagonal join, no ascender, to an anticlockwise letter. Emphasise the spiralling out from the centre.

Join animations

The letter patterns demonstrate the diagonal join, no ascender, to an anticlockwise letter. Talk about the letter patterns: the curve up and over to make the join, then the retrace back in order to finish the second letter.

Challenge word

Click on the toucan to see the challenge word. Children find the target letter pattern in the word. They could also find the letter pattern in a word represented by the artwork.

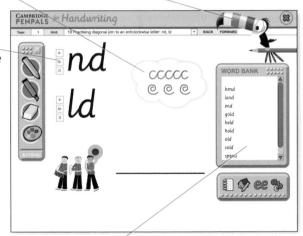

Word bank

Choose a word to discuss. Click on the word to make the diagonal join, no ascender, to an anticlockwise letter grey. Model and discuss the join movement.

Common errors

● not reversing
● diagonal join too steep
● incorrect relative height of letters

Group work

Introduce the page

● Identify the letter patterns at the top of the page.
● Talk about the pictures with the children.
● Ask the children to shut their eyes and listen carefully while you say the words from the Big Book page. If the word you say has an *ld* at the end, children touch their nose; if it has an *nd*, they wave their hands.

Skywriting patterns

● Sky write the patterns shown in the cloud. As you do so, emphasise the fluid movement and the reversal on the first pattern.

Demonstrate the join

● Read the letter patterns and demonstrate the joins.
● Help the children to see how you need to curve up and over to make the join, then stop and trace back over the line in the opposite (anticlockwise) direction before finishing the second letter.
● Emphasise the fluidity of the movement and the relative height of each letter.
● Can the children identify which letter pattern is needed to complete each word? Demonstrate writing the appropriate letter pattern each time.
  Show Me As you write each word, the children copy it. Check that they are joining *nd* or *ld* fluently and accurately each time.

Big Book page 20

Independent work

Watch while the children finger trace the letters and say ❶ the sounds. Make sure they keep their fingers on the page while they trace each of the letter patterns. Ask them to finger trace each letter pattern several times.

Children write the letter patterns in their books. ❷

Read the sentence together, using the picture cue. ❸ Children write the sentence in their books. Ask the children to tell you which letters they are joining in each word. ❺

Encourage the children to practise the pattern in the bottom panel. ❹

Can the children Look, Say, Cover, Write and Check these high-frequency words? Other high-frequency words they could practise are *should* and *would*.

Practice Book page 20

Take away

For additional practice of this join use **PCM 19**.

20 Practising diagonal join, no ascender, to an anticlockwise letter: joining *ng*

Warm up

- Rows of children perform a 'Mexican wave'.
- Children recite the alphabet while tapping each finger in turn on their knees.

CD-ROM

Unit focus: joining *ng*.
Phonic link: consonant digraph **ng**.

Sky writing

Children copy the two patterns to practise the diagonal join, no ascender, to an anticlockwise letter. Emphasise the increase and decrease in the height of the waves.

Join animation

The letter pattern demonstrates the diagonal join, no ascender, to an anticlockwise letter. Talk about the letter patterns: the curve up and over to make the join, then the retrace back in order to finish the second letter.

Challenge word

Click on the toucan to see the challenge word. Children find the target letter pattern in the word. They could also find the letter pattern in a word represented by the artwork.

Word bank

Choose a word to discuss. Click on the word to make the diagonal join to an anticlockwise letter grey. Model and discuss the join movement.

Common errors

- not reversing
- diagonal join too steep
- incorrect length of descender on *g*

Group work

Introduce the page

- Identify the letter pattern.
- Talk about the pictures with the children.

Skywriting patterns

- Sky write the patterns shown in the cloud. As you do so, emphasise the fluid movement and the reversal in the first pattern.

Demonstrate the join

- Read the letter pattern and demonstrate the join.
- Emphasise the fluidity of the movement and the relative height of each letter. Make sure that the descenders on the *g*s are the correct length.
- Read the first sentence together.
- Read the phrase *sing to the king*. Ask children to say the other two phrases.
- Demonstrate writing the letter pattern *ng* each time.
  Show Me As you write each word, the children copy it. Check that they are joining fluently and accurately each time.
- Who can spot something else on the Big Book page that has the **ng** sound in it? (*swing*)

Big Book page 21

Independent work

Watch while the children finger trace the letters and say ❶ the sound. Make sure they keep their fingers on the page while they trace the letter pattern. Ask the children to finger trace the letter pattern several times.

Children write the letter pattern in their books. ❷

Read the sentence together, using the picture cue. ❸ Children write the sentence in their books. Ask them to tell you which letters they are joining in each word.

Encourage the children to practise the pattern in the bottom panel.

Can the children Look, Say, Cover, Write and Check these words?

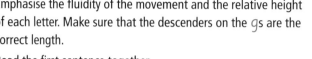

Practice Book page 21

Take away

For additional practice of this join use **PCM 20**.

21 Practising diagonal join, no ascender: joining *ee*

Warm up

- Children make their fingers into buzzing bees and fly them high and low, fast and slow. They should make their bees fly in straight lines, curvy patterns and loops.
- Using each finger in turn, children make their hands tap-dance up the opposite arm.

CD-ROM

Unit focus: joining *ee*.
Phonic link: long vowel phoneme **ee**.

Sky writing

Children copy the two patterns to practise the diagonal join, no ascender, *ee*. Emphasise the flowing, looping movement.

Challenge word

Click on the toucan to see the challenge word. Children find the target letter pattern in the word. They could also find the letter pattern in a word represented by the artwork.

Join animation

The letter pattern demonstrates the diagonal join, no ascender, *ee*. Talk about the letter pattern: the upward slope to make the join and the movement over the top to make the loop.

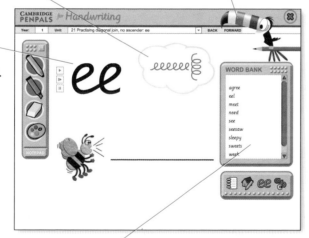

CAMBRIDGE PENPALS *for Handwriting*

Year: 1 Unit: 21 Practising diagonal join, no ascender: ee BACK FORWARD

ee

WORD BANK
agree
eel
meet
need
see
seesaw
sleepy
sweets
week

Word bank

Choose a word to discuss. Click on the word to make the *ee* join grey. Model and discuss the join movement.

Common errors

- incorrect angle of the join to the *e*
- incorrect relative height of the letters

Group work

Introduce the page

- Identify the letter pattern and discuss the pictures.
- Read the text on the Big Book page together.

Skywriting patterns

- Sky write the patterns shown in the cloud. As you do so, emphasise the fluid, looping movement.

Demonstrate the join

- Demonstrate the join.
- Point out the way that the second *e* differs from the first. Emphasise that this is because of the way the join comes into the letter.
  Show Me The children write the letter pattern.
  Get Up and Go Can the children point to the words which contain the letter pattern *ee*?
- Trace over the join each time to demonstrate it.
  Show Me As you trace over the *ee* in each word, the children copy the word.

21 Practising diagonal join, no ascender: joining *ee*

ee   *eeeeee*

Can you see:
a green sheep?
a sneezing bee?
a sleeping queen?
freezing feet?

Big Book page 22

Independent work

Watch while the children finger trace the letters and say **❶** the sound. Make sure they keep their fingers on the page while they trace the letter pattern. Check that the angle of the join to the second *e* is correct each time. Ask the children to finger trace the letter pattern several times.

Children write the letter pattern in their books. **❷**

Read the phrase together, using the picture cue. **❸** Children write the phrase in their books. Ask the children to tell you which letters they are joining in each word.

Encourage the children to practise the pattern in the bottom panel. **❹**

❺

Can the children Look, Say, Cover, Write and Check these high-frequency words?

21 Practising diagonal join, no ascender: joining *ee*

Read and write these words.

Finger trace. Say the sound.
ee   ee   been

Write the letters and the phrase in your book.
ee ee ee ee   seen

three bees on   three
three trees

Practise the pattern.
eeee eeee

Practice Book page 22

Take away

For additional practice of this join use **PCM 21**.

22 Practising diagonal join, no ascender: joining *ai*, *ay*

CD-ROM

Unit focus: joining *ai*, *ay*.
Phonic link: long vowel phoneme **ai**.

Sky writing

Children copy the two patterns to practise the diagonal join, no ascender. Emphasise the regularity of height each time.

Challenge word

Click on the toucan to see the challenge word. Children find the target letter pattern in the word. They could also find the letter pattern in a word represented by the artwork.

Join animations

The letter patterns demonstrate the diagonal join, no ascender, *ai*, *ay*. Talk about the letter patterns and how they require the same join.

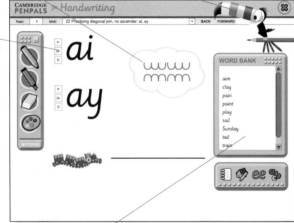

Word bank

Choose a word to discuss. Click on the word to make the *ai* or *ay* join grey. Model and discuss the join movement.

Common errors

- dotting the *i* before the join is complete
- incorrect length of the descender on *y*

Group work

Introduce the page

- Look at the letter patterns and discuss the sound they both make.
- Read the rhyme with the children.

Skywriting patterns

- Sky write the patterns shown in the cloud. As you do so, emphasise the fluid movement.

Demonstrate the join

- Demonstrate how to form the letter patterns at the top of the page.
- Help the children to understand that the same join is needed in both of these letter patterns.
  Show Me The children write each of the letter patterns.
  Get Up and Go Ask children to come up and circle all the *ai* and *ay* patterns within the words.
- Trace over the letter patterns in the raindrops.
- Can the children think of any other rhyming words? (e.g. *ray*, *bay*, *say*; *vain*, *pain*, *gain*) Show the children how to write the words. Then ask them to copy them.

ai ay

Rain, rain,
go away.
Come again
another day.

Big Book page 23

Independent work

Watch while the children finger trace the letters and say the sound. Make sure they keep their fingers on the page while they trace each of the letter patterns. Ask them to finger trace each letter pattern several times.

Children write the letter patterns in their books.

Read the words together, using the picture cues. Children write the words in their books. Ask the children to tell you which letters they are joining in each word.

Encourage the children to practise the pattern in the bottom panel.

Can the children Look, Say, Cover, Write and Check these high-frequency words? Other high-frequency words they could practise are: *play*, *day*, *way* and the days of the week.

Practice Book page 23

Take away

For additional practice of this join use **PCM 22**.

23 Practising diagonal join, no ascender: joining *ime, ine*

Warm up

- 👋 Children work in pairs and clap their hands against their partner's hands. Then they clap normally themselves. Can they make a sequence using the different kinds of clap?
- 👋 Children rub their hands together very, very fast and then shake their hands above their heads. Repeat.

CD-ROM

Unit focus: joining *ime, ine*.
Phonic link: long vowel phoneme **ie**.

Sky writing

Children copy the two patterns to practise the diagonal join, no ascender. Emphasise the symmetry of the patterns.

Challenge word

Click on the toucan to see the challenge word. Children find the target letter pattern in the word. They could also find the letter pattern in a word represented by the artwork.

Join animations

The letter patterns demonstrate the diagonal join, no ascender, *ime, ine*. Talk about the letter patterns and how they require the same join.

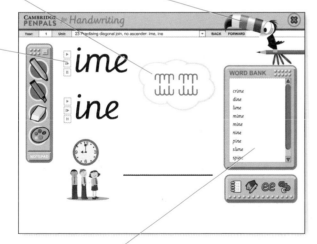

Word bank

Choose a word to discuss. Click on the word to make the *ime* or *ine* join grey. Model and discuss the join movement.

Common errors

- lifting the pencil before the letter pattern is complete
- incorrect spacing between the letters
- letters not of a consistent size

Group work

Introduce the page

- Read the letter patterns at the top of the page together.
- Read the sentence with the children and discuss the picture.

Skywriting patterns

- Sky write the patterns shown in the cloud. As you do so, emphasise the fluid movement.

Demonstrate the join

- Demonstrate the joins.
- Remind the children that they should not take their pencil off the page until the joined letter pattern is complete. They should dot the i only after finishing the whole letter pattern.
  Show Me Children write each of the letter patterns.
- Demonstrate tracing over the letter patterns in *time* and *line*.
  Show Me Children write the words *time* and *line*.
- Can the children think of any other rhyming words? (e.g. *mine, pine, fine; dime, mime, chime*) Show the children how to write the words. Then ask them to copy them.

Independent work

Watch while the children finger trace the letters and say the ❶ sounds. Make sure they keep their fingers on the page while they trace each of the letter patterns. Check that the is are only dotted after the letter pattern is complete. Ask the children to finger trace each letter pattern several times.

Children write the letter patterns in their books. ❷

Read the phrases together, using the picture cues. ❸ Children write the phrases in their books. Ask the children to tell you which letters they are joining in each word.

Encourage the children to practise the pattern in the bottom panel. ❹

Can the children Look, Say, Cover, Write and Check these words? ❺

Take away

For additional practice of this join use **PCM 23**.

Big Book page 24

Practice Book page 24

Warm up

- Children jump and hop up and down.
- Children draw a spiral on their palm with different fingers.

CD-ROM

Unit focus: joining *op*, *oy*.
Phonic link: reading and writing CVC words.

Sky writing

Children copy the two patterns to introduce the horizontal join, no ascender. Emphasise the horizontal lines of the patterns.

Join animations

The letter patterns demonstrate the horizontal join, no ascender. Talk about the letter patterns and how they require the same join.

Challenge word

Click on the toucan to see the challenge word. Children find the target letter pattern in the word. They could also find the letter pattern in a word represented by the artwork.

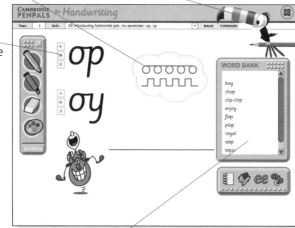

Word bank

Choose a word to discuss. Click on the word to make the horizontal join, no ascender, grey. Model and discuss the join movement.

Common errors

- overshooting on the horizontal line
- inaccurate retracing of the vertical on p
- incorrect orientation of y
- going too far back or not far back enough on the formation of the o

---

Group work

Introduce the page

- Identify the letter patterns at the top of the page and talk about what is happening in the pictures.

Skywriting patterns

- Sky write the patterns shown in the cloud, emphasising the horizontal line.

Demonstrate the join

- Demonstrate the join by tracing over the letter patterns at the top of the page.
- Talk about the join, pointing out that this join is a straight line from the top of the first letter.
- Focus on the length of the descenders, and the curve of the y to the left.
  Show Me Children write the letter patterns.
  Get Up and Go Ask the children to come up and point to the letter pattern needed to finish each of the words.
- Write in the correct letter pattern to finish each of the words.
  Show Me Children copy the words.
- Think of and write up some rhyming words (e.g. *cop*, *mop*, *top*, *Roy*) for children to copy.
- Can any children see which words could also end with the other letter pattern? (*top*, *bop*)

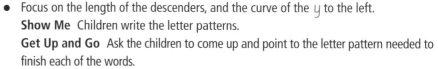

Big Book page 25

Independent work

Watch while the children finger trace the letters and say **①** the sounds. Make sure they keep their fingers on the page while they trace each of the letter patterns. Check that the horizontal join is carefully completed. Ask the children to finger trace each letter pattern several times.

Children write the letter patterns in their books. **②**

Read the words together, using the picture cues. **③**
Children write the words in their books. Ask the children to tell you which letters they are joining in each word.

Encourage the children to practise the pattern in the bottom panel.

Can the children Look, Say, Cover, Write and Check these words?

Practice Book page 25

Take away

For additional practice of this join use **PCM 24**.

Warm up

- 👋 Using their hands, children perform the actions to *Here Is The Church, Here Is The Steeple* (see **Foundation 1 CD**, track 17; **Teacher's Book**, page 46).
- 👋 Children sing *Here Is The Church, Here Is The Steeple* again, but this time perform the actions on a large scale, using their whole bodies.

CD-ROM

Unit focus: joining *one*, *ome*.
Phonic link: long vowel phoneme **oa**.

Sky writing

Children copy the two patterns to practise the horizontal join, no ascender. Emphasise the horizontal lines of the patterns.

Challenge word

Click on the toucan to see the challenge word. Children find the target letter pattern in the word. They could also find the letter pattern in a word represented by the artwork.

Join animations

The letter patterns demonstrate the horizontal join, no ascender. Talk about the letter patterns and how they require the same join.

Word bank

Choose a word to discuss. Click on the word to make the horizontal join, no ascender, grey. Model and discuss the join movement.

Common errors

- clockwise rather than anticlockwise movement to form the o
- too much space between the letters

Group work

Introduce the page

- Read the phrase and discuss the picture with the children.

Skywriting patterns

- Sky write the patterns shown in the cloud. In the first pattern, emphasise the horizontal line coming from the top of the circle.

Demonstrate the join

- Demonstrate tracing over the letter patterns at the top of the page.
- Talk about the join, pointing out that this join is a straight line from the top of the first letter.
  Show Me Children write the letter patterns.
  Get Up and Go Ask children to come up and circle the *one* and *ome* letter patterns in the words.
- Ask children to think of some rhyming words (e.g. *dome; phone, bone*). Model writing these words for the children to copy.

Big Book page 26

Independent work

Watch while the children finger trace the letters and say ❶ the sounds. Make sure they keep their fingers on the page while they trace each of the letter patterns. Check that the horizontal join is carefully completed. Ask the children to finger trace each letter pattern several times.

Children write the letter patterns in their books. ❷

Read the sentence together, using the picture cue. ❸ Children write the sentence in their books. Ask the children to tell you which letters they are joining in each word.

Encourage the children to practise the pattern in the bottom panel.

    Can the children Look, Say, Cover, Write and Check these high-frequency words?

Practice Book page 26

Take away

For additional practice of this join use **PCM 25**.

26 Introducing horizontal join, no ascender, to an anticlockwise letter: joining *oa*, *og*

Warm up

✋ Children make big spiral movements in the air with their arms. When you call out 'Reverse!', they make the movements in the opposite direction.

✋ Demonstrate how to sky write a succession of joined *c*s and tell children that these are waves on the sea. Call out 'weather reports' for them to make bigger or smaller wave patterns.

CD-ROM

Unit focus: joining *oa*, *og*.

Phonic links: long vowel phoneme **oa**; reading and writing CVC words.

Sky writing

Children copy the two patterns to introduce the horizontal join, no ascender, to an anticlockwise letter. Emphasise the flow of the movements and the horizontal lines in the second pattern.

Join animations

The letter patterns demonstrate the horizontal join, no ascender, to an anticlockwise letter. Talk about the letter patterns: the horizontal line to make the join and begin the top of the second letter, then the retrace back in order to finish the second letter.

Challenge word

Click on the toucan to see the challenge word. Children find the target letter pattern in the word. They could also find the letter pattern in a word represented by the artwork.

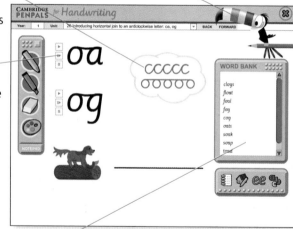

Word bank

Choose a word to discuss. Click on the word to make the horizontal join, no ascender, grey. Model and discuss the join movement.

Common errors

- overshooting on the horizontal line
- inaccurate spacing of the letters
- incorrect orientation of *g*
- going too far back or not far back enough on the formation of the *o*

Group work

Introduce the page

- Identify the letter patterns at the top of the page and talk about the pictures with the children.

Skywriting patterns

- Sky write the patterns shown in the cloud, emphasising the horizontal lines in the second pattern.

Demonstrate the join

- Demonstrate the join by tracing over the letter patterns at the top of the page.
- Talk about the join, reminding children that it is a straight line from the top of the first letter. Help the children to see how you need to go straight across to make the join, then stop and go back to make the *a* or the *g*.
- Focus on the length of the descender, and the curve of the *g* to the left. **Show Me** Children write the letter patterns.
- Model tracing over the *oa* and *og* letter patterns in the words. **Show Me** Children copy the words.
- Ask the children to think of some rhyming words (e.g. *boat, float, moat; fog, hog, jog*). Model writing these words for the children to copy.

Big Book page 27

Independent work

Watch while the children finger trace the letters and say ❶ the sounds. Make sure they keep their fingers on the page while they trace each of the letter patterns. Check that the horizontal join is carefully completed. Ask the children to finger trace each letter pattern several times.

Children write the letter patterns in their books. ❷

Read the phrase together, using the picture cue. ❸ Children write the phrase in their books. Ask the children to tell you which letters they are joining in each word.

Encourage the children to practise the pattern in the bottom panel. ❹

Can the children Look, Say, Cover, Write and Check these words? ❺

Practice Book page 27

Take away

For additional practice of this join use **PCM 26**.

Warm up

- Children put the heels of their hands together and 'clap' each pair of fingers in turn.
- Children finger trace letters on to each other's backs. When one child has finished a letter, their partner then traces the letter they thought they felt on to the first child's back.

CD-ROM

Unit focus: joining *wa, wo*.
Phonic link: long vowel phoneme **ai**.

Sky writing

Children copy the two patterns to practise the horizontal join, no ascender, to an anticlockwise letter. Emphasise the regularity of the movements.

Challenge word

Click on the toucan to see the challenge word. Children find the target letter pattern in the word. They could also find the letter pattern in a word represented by the artwork.

Join animations

The letter patterns demonstrate the horizontal join, no ascender, to an anticlockwise letter. Talk about the letter patterns: the horizontal line to make the join and begin the top of the second letter, then the retrace back in order to finish the second letter.

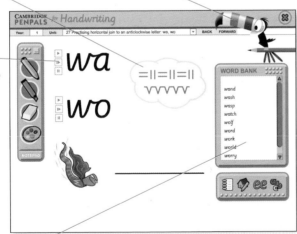

Word bank

Choose a word to discuss. Click on the word to make the horizontal join to an anticlockwise letter grey. Model and discuss the join movement.

Common errors

- going too far with the horizontal line
- not closing the top of the *a* or the *o* and finishing it off afterwards *a   a*
- clockwise rather than anticlockwise movement to form the *o*
- continuing the exit stroke of the *o* (don't worry too much about this as it will prepare for further joins later)

Group work

Introduce the page

- Identify the letter patterns at the top of the page and talk about the pictures with the children. Read the captions.

Skywriting patterns

- Sky write the patterns shown in the cloud.

Demonstrate the join

- Demonstrate the join by tracing over the letter patterns at the top of the page.
- Remind children that the join is a straight line from the top of the first letter. Point out that the letters are the same height. Help the children to see how you need to go straight across to make the join, then stop and go back to make the *a* or the *o*.
  Show Me Children write the letter patterns.
  Get Up and Go Ask children to come up and point to the *wa* and *wo* patterns in *worried worm, warm worm* and *wacky worm*.
- Model tracing over and writing the *wa* and *wo* letter patterns in *water worm, waiting worm* and *wonder worm*.
  Show Me Children copy the words.

Big Book page 28

Independent work

Watch while the children finger trace the letters and say ➊ the sounds. Make sure they keep their fingers on the page while they trace each of the letter patterns. Check that the horizontal join is carefully completed. Ask the children to finger trace each letter pattern several times.

Children write the letter patterns in their books. ➋

Read the phrase together, using the picture cue. ➌ Children write the phrase in their books. Ask the children to tell you which letters they are joining in each word.

Encourage the children to practise the pattern in the bottom panel.

Can the children Look, Say, Cover, Write and Check these high-frequency words?

Practice Book page 28

Take away

For additional practice of this join use **PCM 27**.

Warm up

- 👋 Children sing *I Can Play On The Big Bass Drum* and mime the actions.
- 👋 Children play Show Me with various parts of their hands, indicating each one without pointing (e.g. wiggle fingers, form hand into a fist to show knuckles, hold palms up).

CD-ROM

Unit focus: joining *ol, ot*.
Phonic link: reading and writing CVC words.

Sky writing

Children copy the two patterns to practise the horizontal join to an ascender. Emphasise the flow in the first pattern.

Challenge word

Click on the toucan to see the challenge word. Children find the target letter pattern in the word. They could also find the letter pattern in a word represented by the artwork.

Join animations

The letter patterns demonstrate the horizontal join to an ascender. Talk about the letter patterns: the horizontal line to make the join go up to the top of the second letter and then down. The cross on the *t* is the last stroke.

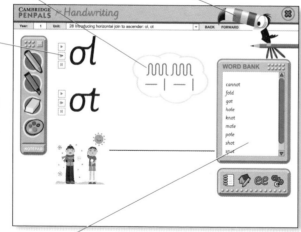

Word bank

Choose a word to discuss. Click on the word to make the horizontal join to an ascender grey. Model and discuss the join movement.

Common errors

- loop on the top of the o
- ascender diagonal rather than horizontal
- join too long

Group work

Introduce the page

- Identify the letter patterns at the top of the page and talk about the picture with the children.

Skywriting patterns

- Sky write the patterns shown in the cloud.

Demonstrate the join

- Demonstrate the join by tracing over the letter patterns at the top of the page.
- Remind children that, once again, the join starts from the top of the first letter, but this time it swings across and up to the top of the second letter.
- Point out that you don't put the cross bar on the *t* until you have finished the join.
  Show Me Children write the letter patterns.
- Model tracing over the *ol* and *ot* letter patterns in *told* and *not*.
  Get Up and Go Ask children to point to the letter patterns needed to fill the gaps in *cold* and *hot*.
- Model writing the letter patterns in the gaps.
  Show Me Children copy the words featuring the letter patterns.

Big Book page 29

Independent work

Watch while the children finger trace the letters and say the sounds. Make sure they keep their fingers on the page while they trace each of the letter patterns. Check that the horizontal join is carefully completed. Make sure that the children are tracing the *o*s in an anticlockwise direction and that the *t* is not crossed until the join is complete. Ask them to finger trace each letter pattern several times. **❶**

Children write the letter patterns in their books. **❷**

Read the phrase together, using the picture cue. **❸**
Children write the phrase in their books. Ask the children to tell you which letters they are joining in each word.

Encourage the children to practise the pattern in the bottom panel. **❹**

Can the children Look, Say, Cover, Write and Check these high-frequency words? **❺**

Practice Book page 29

Take away

For additional practice of this join use **PCM 28**.

29 Practising horizontal join to ascender: joining *wh, oh*

Warm up

- Children roll their shoulders backwards and forwards, shrug both shoulders up to their ears, then shrug their right and left shoulders independently.
- Children recite the alphabet, touching each finger in turn to the end of their nose as they do so.

CD-ROM

Unit focus: joining *wh, oh*.
Phonic links: consonant digraph **wh**; long vowel phoneme **oa**.

Sky writing

Children copy the two patterns to practise the horizontal join to an ascender. Emphasise the flow of these patterns: one curved, the other straight.

Challenge word

Click on the toucan to see the challenge word. Children find the target letter pattern in the word. They could also find the letter pattern in a word represented by the artwork.

Join animations

The letter patterns demonstrate the horizontal join to an ascender. Talk about the letter patterns: the horizontal line to make the join go up to the top of the second letter and then down.

Word bank

Choose a word to discuss. Click on the word to make the horizontal join to an ascender grey. Model and discuss the join movement.

Common errors

- incorrect spacing between the letters
- join diagonal rather than horizontal
- disproportionate letter sizes
- going too far up on the ascender

Group work

Introduce the page

- Identify the letter patterns at the top of the page and talk about the picture with the children.

Skywriting patterns

- Sky write the patterns shown in the cloud. Emphasise the diagonal swing up on the second pattern.

Demonstrate the join

- Demonstrate the join by tracing over the letter patterns at the top of the page.
- Remind children that once again the join starts from the top of the first letter, and then swings across and up to the top of the second letter.
  Show Me Children write the letter patterns.
- Model tracing over the *oh* and *wh* letter patterns in the words.
  Show Me Children copy the words.

Big Book page 30

Independent work

Watch while the children finger trace the letters and say ❶ the sounds. Make sure they keep their fingers on the page while they trace each of the letter patterns. Check that the horizontal join is carefully completed. Ask the children to finger trace each letter pattern several times.

Children write the letter patterns in their books. ❷

Read the phrase together, using the picture cue. ❸
Children write the phrase in their books. Ask the children to tell you which letters they are joining in each word. ❺

Encourage the children to practise the pattern in the bottom panel. ❹

Can the children Look, Say, Cover, Write and Check these high-frequency words?

Practice Book page 30

Take away

For additional practice of this join use **PCM 29**.

Warm up

☝ Children mime climbing a ladder.

☝ Which skywriting patterns have the children enjoyed? They can practise writing their favourites on the palm of their hand.

CD-ROM

Unit focus: joining *of*, *if*.
Phonic link: the terms *vowel* and *consonant*.

Sky writing

Children copy the two patterns to practise joins to *f*. Emphasise the flow of these patterns: one curved, the other straight.

Join animations

The letter patterns demonstrate the joins to an ascender, to an anticlockwise letter, *f*. Talk about the letter patterns: the upward lines (one from the baseline and one from the top of the *o*), to make the joins up to the top of the *f*.

Challenge word

Click on the toucan to see the challenge word. Children find the target letter pattern in the word. They could also find the letter pattern in a word represented by the artwork.

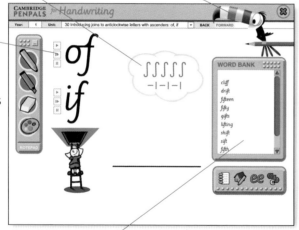

Word bank

Choose a word to discuss. Click on the word to make the horizontal or diagonal join to an anticlockwise letter grey. Model and discuss the join movement.

Common errors

- inaccurate retracing on the reversal
- join diagonal rather than horizontal
- disproportionate letter sizes
- descender of the *f* above the line *of*

Group work

Introduce the page

- Identify the letter patterns at the top of the page and talk about the picture with the children.
- Ask the children: which letters in *of* and *if* are vowels? Which are consonants?

Skywriting patterns

- Sky write the patterns shown in the cloud. Emphasise the curves at the top and bottom of the first pattern.

Demonstrate the joins

- Demonstrate the joins by tracing over the letter pattern at the top of the page.
- Remind children that the *of* join starts from the top of the *o* and swings across and up to the top of the *f*. The *if* join starts from the flick of the *i* and swings up to the top of the *f*. Next, you curve up and over to make the join, then you stop and trace back over the line in the opposite (anticlockwise) direction before finishing the *f*.
- Remind children that you don't cross the *f* until the join is complete. **Show Me** Children write the letter patterns.
- Note that the *of* join provides another opportunity to practise the diagonal join to an anticlockwise letter with an ascender.
- Model tracing over the letter patterns in grey. Then model writing *of* in the gap in *coffee*. **Show Me** Children copy the words.

Big Book page 31

Independent work

Watch while the children finger trace the letters and say the sound. Make sure they keep their fingers on the page while they trace the letter pattern. Check that the horizontal join and reversal are carefully completed, and that children do not cross the *f* until the join is complete. Ask them to finger trace the letter pattern several times. ❶

Children write the letter pattern in their books. ❷

Read the sentence together, using the picture cue. ❸ Children write the sentence in their books. Ask the children to tell you which letters they are joining in each word. ❺

Encourage the children to practise the pattern in the bottom panel. ❹

Can the children Look, Say, Cover, Write and Check these words?

Practice Book page 31

Take away

For additional practice of this join use **PCM 30**.

Warm up

👋 Children practise their favourite skywriting pattern.

👋 Children write simple CVC words with their finger on each other's backs and try to guess the word.

NB: The Big Book page in this unit offers an opportunity to consolidate all the types of join covered this year. The results of children's Practice Book work can be used as an end-of-year assessment to measure their progress and identify targets for the coming year.

Group work

Unit focus: assessment.
Phonic link: high-frequency words.

Introduce the page

● Explain to children that this unit will give them a chance to recap what they have learnt this year, and to see how well their handwriting has come along.

Demonstrate the join

● Demonstrate the joins in the first column by tracing over the letter patterns in grey.
 Show Me Children practise writing the letter patterns.

● Think of a CVC word which features the letter pattern – encourage children to offer suggestions. Model how to write that word in the second column.

● For *of* and *if* children will need to add a letter to the beginning <u>and</u> the end of the letter pattern to make a word.

Big Book page 32

Independent work

Watch while the children finger trace the letters and say the sounds. Make sure they keep their fingers on the page while they trace the letter patterns.

Children write the words in their books. Check that all the joins are secure, and ask children to repeat any which appear shaky.

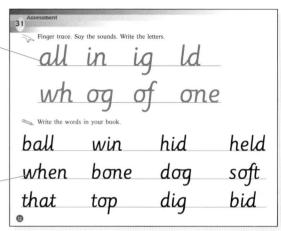

Practice Book page 32

Common errors

● When assessing children's work, look out for any of the errors already mentioned in this section which may still be cropping up.

UNIT 1 Letter formation practice: long ladder family

Name

Date

Trace the letters.
Say the sounds.

l t j y i u

 l t j y i u

Write the missing long ladder letters.

ca____

 ____ion

 mbrella

elly

Penpals for Handwriting: Y1

© Gill Budgell (Frattempo) and Kate Ruttle 2009

UNIT 2 Letter formation practice: one-armed robot family

Name

Date

Trace the letters.
Say the sounds.

r n m h b p k

 r n m h b p k

Write the missing one-armed robot letters.

un____

____all

e____

par____

Penpals for Handwriting: Y1

© Gill Budgell (Frattempo) and Kate Ruttle 2009

UNIT 3 Letter formation practice: curly caterpillar family

Name

Date

Trace the letters.
Say the sounds.

a c o g q d e f s

Write the missing curly caterpillar letters.

_ueen

_n

_un

_g

UNIT 4 Letter formation practice: zig-zag monster family

Name

Date

Trace the letters.
Say the sounds.

z x w v

Write the missing zig-zag monster letters.

_et

_ebra

si_

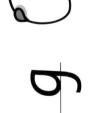

an_

UNIT 5 Practising the vowels: *i*

Name .... Date ....

Trace and write the letters. Say the sounds.

i   *i*   _____

p   *p*   _____

l   *l*   _____

Write the missing letters. Read the words.

 l _____

l p s _____

 p _____ n

t _____ n

 d _____ d

---

UNIT 6 Practising the vowels: *u*

Name .... Date ....

Trace and write the letters. Say the sounds.

u   *u*   _____

s   *s*   _____

Write the missing letters. Read the words.

j *g* _____

 _____ g

 y _____ m

 _____ n

 m _____

2 + 2 = _____

UNIT 7 Practising the vowels: *a*

Name ....   Date ....

Trace and write the letters. Say the sounds.

a   *a*   *r*   *d*

Write the missing letters. Read the words.

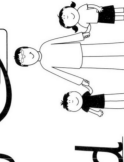

c p __

b g

t __

d __ d

UNIT 8 Practising the vowels: *o*

Name ....   Date ....

Trace and write the letters. Say the sounds.

o   *o*   *f*   *f*   *p*

Write the missing letters. Read the words.

r d __

h __ t

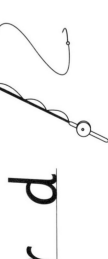

x __

__ p

Practising the vowels: *e*

Name

Date

Trace and write the letters. Say the sounds.

e_ _ _ n_ _ _ h_ _ _

Write the missing letters. Read the words.

l _ g

t _ n

t _

_ _ n

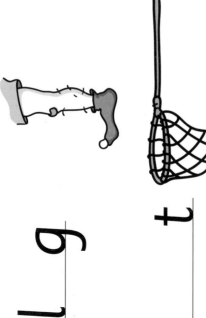

Penpals for Handwriting: Y1

© Gill Budgell (Frattempo) and Kate Ruttle 2009

Letter formation practice: capital letters

Name

Date

Trace and write the letters. Say the sounds.

D_ _ _ H_ _ _ L_ _ _ P_ _ _ T_ _ _ X_ _ _ Z

Write the missing letters. Always start at the top.

B _ D _ F _ H

J _ L _ N _ P

R _ T _ V _ X _ Z

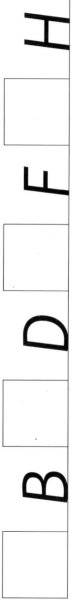

Penpals for Handwriting: Y1

© Gill Budgell (Frattempo) and Kate Ruttle 2009

UNIT 11 Introducing diagonal join to ascender: joining *at, all*

Name _____ Date _____

Trace and write the joined letters. Say the sounds.

at   *all*

Finish the words. Remember to join!

b _____

m _____

b _____

w _____

UNIT 12 Practising diagonal join to ascender: joining *th*

Name _____ Date _____

Trace and write the joined letters. Say the sound.

th th

Trace and write the words. Remember to join the *th*!

the the

then then

they they

this this

UNIT 13 Practising diagonal join to ascender: *joining ch*

Name

Date

Trace and write the joined letters. Say the sound.

ch ch

Finish the words. Remember to join!

_eese

in_

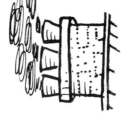

_op

_imney

Penpals for Handwriting: Y1

UNIT 14 Practising diagonal join to ascender: *joining cl*

Name

Date

Trace and write the joined letters. Say the sound.

cl cl

Finish the words. Remember to join!

_ock

_othes

_ap

_ip

Penpals for Handwriting: Y1

UNIT 15 Introducing diagonal join, no ascender: joining *in, im*

Name

Date

Trace and write the joined letters. Say the sounds.

im   in   in

Trace and finish the words. Remember to join!

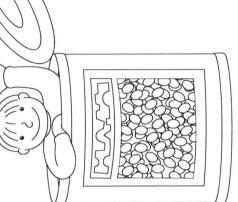

Tim is in

the t ____ .

UNIT 16 Practising diagonal join, no ascender: joining *cr, tr, dr*

Name

Date

Trace and write the joined letters. Say the sounds.

cr   tr   dr

Finish the words. Remember to join!

ee ____

____ ab

____ um

UNIT 17 Practising diagonal join, no ascender: joining *lp, mp*

Name ....

Date ....

Trace and write the joined letters. Say the sounds.

lp　*mp*

Write a rhyming word. Remember to join!

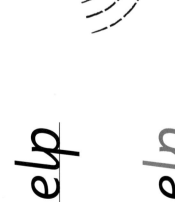

yelp

help

camp

_____

UNIT 18 Introducing diagonal join, no ascender, to an anticlockwise letter: joining *id, ig*

Name ....

Date ....

Trace and write the joined letters. Say the sounds.

id　*ig*

Finish the rhyming words. Remember to join!

did　*hid*

k___　*l___*

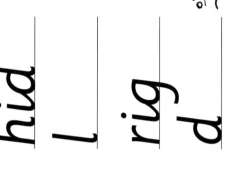

big　*rig*

w___　*d___*

UNIT 19 Practising diagonal join, no ascender, to an anticlockwise letter: joining *nd, ld*

Name .... Date ....

Trace and write the joined letters. Say the sounds.

nd   *nd*

ld   *ld*

Sort the words into sets. Remember to join!

nd _____ _____ _____

ld _____ _____ _____

sand   hold
cold   band
told   hand

Penpals for Handwriting: Y1

UNIT 20 Practising diagonal join, no ascender, to an anticlockwise letter: joining *ng*

Name .... Date ....

Trace and write the joined letters. Say the sound.

ng   *ng*   *ng*

Finish the rhyming words. Remember to join!

sing

r___ *rang*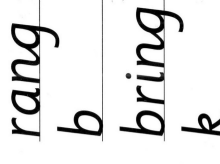

long

s___

b___ *bring*

k___

Penpals for Handwriting: Y1

Practising diagonal join, no ascender: joining *ee*

Name .... Date ....

Trace and write the joined letters. Say the sound.

ee *ee* _____

Finish the rhyme. Remember to join!

What can you s___?

A happy b___!

Practising diagonal join, no ascender: joining *ai, ay*

Name .... Date ....

Trace and write the joined letters. Say the sound.

ai _____

ay _____

Finish the rhyming words. Remember to join!

way   day

h___   pl___

pain   rail

r___   sn___

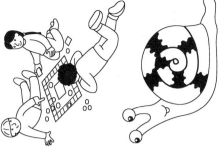

UNIT 23 Practising diagonal join, no ascender: joining *ime, ine*

Name .... Date ....

Trace and write the joined letters. Say the sounds.

ime *ine*

Finish the rhyme. Remember to join!

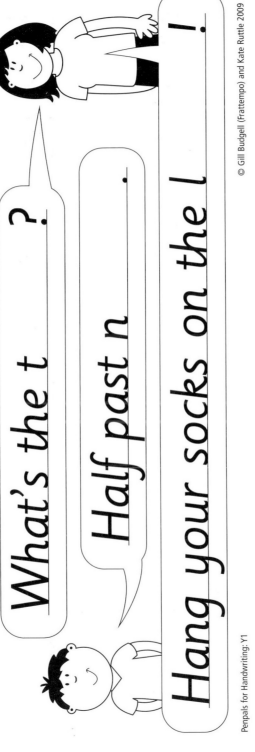

What's the t ?

Half past n .

Hang your socks on the l !

UNIT 24 Introducing horizontal join, no ascender: joining *op, oy*

Name .... Date ....

Trace and write the joined letters. Say the sounds.

op *oy*

Finish the sentence. Remember to join!

Hop to the toy

sh , b !

UNIT 25

Practising horizontal join, no ascender: joining *one*, *ome*

Name _____ Date _____

Trace and write the joined letters. Say the sounds.

one *ome*

Finish the words. Remember to join!

b_____  thr_____

h_____ st_____

UNIT 26

Introducing horizontal join, no ascender, to an anticlockwise letter: joining *oa*, *og*

Name _____ Date _____

Trace and write the joined letters. Say the sounds.

oa *og*

Finish the words. Remember to join!

b_____  fr_____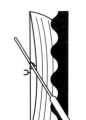

t_____ g_____  d_____

UNIT 27 Practising horizontal join, no ascender, to an anticlockwise letter: joining *wa*, *wo*

Name .... Date ....

Trace and write the joined letters. Say the sounds.

wa   *wo*

Sort the words into sets. Remember to join!

water work worm want walk would

wa _____

wo _____

UNIT 28 Introducing horizontal join to ascender: joining *ot*, *ot*

Name .... Date ....

Trace and write the joined letters. Say the sounds.

ot   *ot*

Finish the words. Remember to join!

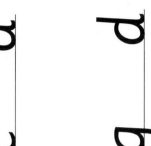

h _____   c _____ d

p _____   g _____ d

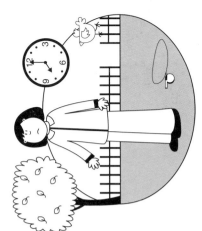

UNIT 29 Practising horizontal join to ascender: joining *wh, oh*

Name _____ Date _____

Trace and write the joined letters. Say the sounds.

wh   *oh*

Finish the words. Remember to join!

Where, oh   *ere*

is my   *istle?*

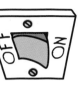

Penpals for Handwriting: Y1

 © Gill Budgell (Frattempo) and Kate Ruttle 2009

UNIT 30 Introducing horizontal and diagonal joins, to ascender, to an anticlockwise letter: joining *of, if*

Name _____ Date _____

Trace and write the joined letters.

of   *if*

Finish the words. Remember to join!

c _ fee   cl   f

g _ t   f

Penpals for Handwriting: Y1

© Gill Budgell (Frattempo) and Kate Ruttle 2009

a b c d e f g h i j k l m n o p q r s t u v w x y z

Penpals
writing mat

for right-handers

A B C D E F G H I J K L M N O P Q R S T U V W X Y Z

Penpals for Handwriting   © Gill Budgell (Frattempo) and Kate Ruttle 2009

A B C D E F G H I J K L M N O P Q R S T U V W X Y Z

for left-handers

Penpals
writing mat

a b c d e f g h i j k l m n o p q r s t u v w x y z